Penguin Critical Studies
Advisory Editors:
Stephen Coote and Bryan Loughrey

John Milton

Paradise Lost

Peter Weston

Penguin Books

PENGUIN BOOKS

Published by the Penguin Group
27 Wrights Lane, London W8 5TZ, England
Viking Penguin Inc., 40 West 23rd Street, New York, New York 10010, USA
Penguin Books Australia Ltd, Ringwood, Victoria, Australia
Penguin Books Canada Ltd, 2801 John Street, Markham, Ontario, Canada L3R 1B4
Penguin Books (NZ) Ltd, 182–190 Wairau Road, Auckland 10, New Zealand

Penguin Books Ltd, Registered Offices: Harmondsworth, Middlesex, England

First published as a Penguin Masterstudy 1987
Reprinted as a Penguin Critical Study 1990
10 9 8 7 6 5 4 3 2 1

Made and printed in Great Britain by
Richard Clay Ltd, Bungay, Suffolk
Filmset in Monophoto Times

Contents

I Preliminaries

1 Reading an Epic

Can the same words in a different order mean the same thing?

Paradise Lost is not a difficult poem.
A difficult poem *Paradise Lost* is not.

The first statement might seem more 'natural', in the sense of more like everyday speech, but the second, precisely through being less 'natural', is much more emphatic. Thus a deviation from the ordinary patterns of everyday language can produce an interesting effect, and even a poetic effect, within a simple five-stress line, such as those above.

Examples of this simple device can be found on every page of *Paradise Lost*. When Milton writes of Satan's followers in hell that they

... observed
Their dread commander: he above the rest
In shape and gesture proudly eminent
Stood like a tower; ...

(I. 588–91)

the delaying of the main verb 'stood' for more than one line, and its location at the start of its line where it displaces the normally unstressed first syllable, give much more emphasis to Satan's stature, and prepare us emotionally for the simile of the tower. In addition, the use of apposition ('their dread commander: he', rather than the more everyday 'their dread commander, who') provides a momentary pause, or caesura, which serves as a rhythmic emphasis of Satan's impressive separateness. Again, for a quite different effect of Milton's displacement of 'natural' word order, consider the description of Satan's choice of the serpent as the creature which he will use for the seduction of Eve. Abandoning the usual structure 'he chose him', Milton uses 'him ... he chose', and thus manages to emphasize not only the finality and fitness of the decision, but also Satan's tortuous internal debate which led to the decision:

Him after long debate, irresolute
Of thoughts revolved, his final sentence [i.e. 'judgment'] *chose*

> *Fit vessel, fittest imp of fraud, in whom*
> *To enter, ...*
>
> (IX. 87–90)

Starting the line and the sentence with the object, 'him' (the serpent), has the dramatic effect of a finger pointing, and the heavily stressed first words two lines later, 'fit vessel', force a contrast between the positive decision and the long irresolute debate beforehand. But beyond this, there is a complex ambiguity hovering around the lines, since they contain a biblical echo, of the verse in Romans 9:22 in which reference is made to God's enduring 'with much longsuffering the vessels of wrath fitted to destruction'. So Milton's unattached placing of 'his' in the middle of the line aptly reinforces the ambiguity of who is really choosing whom, as vessel for what, as a 'final sentence', Satan or God.

The unusual placing of the object of a sentence before the main verb for emphasis can be used by Milton with a quite different effect. Consider Sin's story, of how Death, her son, lustfully chased her through hell:

> *... I fled, and cried out Death;*
> *Hell trembled at the hideous name, and sighed*
> *From all her caves, and back resounded Death.*
> *I fled, but he pursued (though more, it seems,*
> *Inflamed with lust than rage) and swifter far*
> *Me overtook his mother all dismayed, ...*
>
> (II. 787–92)

The alliteration of that last line clarifies the apposition of 'me' and 'mother dismayed', which are forcibly separated by the verb 'overtook', and so the suddenness and horror of the rape is enacted by the syntax with far more telling effect than 'Overtook me, his all-dismayed mother' would have done, for instance. The previous echo of 'Death' and the repetition of 'I fled' are here brought to a grisly climax. The consequences, however, are long-drawn-out, and the extended construction which follows illustrates Milton's prescription for 'true musical delight', which consists in part of 'the sense variously drawn out from one verse [i.e. 'line'] into another'. Though it is hardly everyday English, it is not at all hard to follow, and terminates climactically with an inversion in three thumping monosyllables: 'none I find':

> [He] *in embraces forcible and foul*
> *Ingendering with me, of that rape begot*
> *These yelling monsters that with ceaseless cry*
> *Surround me, as thou sawest, hourly conceived,*

And hourly born, with sorrow infinite
To me, for when they list into the womb
That bred them they return, and howl and gnaw
My bowels, their repast; then bursting forth
Afresh with conscious terrors vex me round,
That rest or intermission none I find.

(II. 793–802)

(Compare 'So that I find no rest or intermission', which, though sounding more 'natural', is quite without the force of Milton's line.)

These are all fairly straightforward examples of the kinds of effects that Milton can produce with departures from the usual order of everyday language. Such language makes the poem impressive rather than 'difficult', and the supposed difficulty of the poem is usually no more than a transient first impression. Being without rhymes, *Paradise Lost* must rely for its effects on such other strategies of diction, syntax, and rhythm which set it apart from prose. Dr Johnson, in his *Life* of Milton, commented: 'He that thinks himself capable of astonishing may write blank verse, but those that hope only to please must condescend to rhyme.' Milton frequently astonishes. In illustration, consider the variety of Satan's language in *Paradise Lost*. He can speak with awesome defiance (addressing Death, who blocks his exit from hell):

Whence and what art thou, execrable shape,
That darest, though grim and terrible, advance
Thy miscreated front athwart my way
To yonder gates? Through them I mean to pass,
That be assured, without leave asked of thee:
Retire, or taste thy folly, and learn by proof,
Hell-born, not to contend with spirits of heaven.

(II. 681–7)

– or with penetrating introspection (on landing on earth for the first time):

Me miserable! Which way shall I fly
Infinite wrath, and infinite despair?
Which way I fly is hell; my self am hell;
And in the lowest deep a lower deep
Still threatening to devour me opens wide,
To which the hell I suffer seems a heaven.
O then at last relent: is there no place
Left for repentance, none for pardon left?
None left but by submission; and that word

Disdain forbids me, and my dread of shame
Among the spirits beneath, whom I seduced
With other promises and other vaunts
Than to submit, boasting I could subdue
The omnipotent . . .

(IV. 73–86)

– or with hauteur (to his juniors, when caught by them at the ear of Eve):

Know ye not then said Satan, filled with scorn,
Know ye not me? Ye knew me once no mate
For you, there sitting where ye durst not soar;
Not to know me argues your selves unknown,
The lowest of your throng; or if ye know,
Why ask ye, and superfluous begin
Your message, like to end as much in vain?

(IV. 827–33)

– or with persuasive compression (to Eve, near the climax of her seduction):

Queen of this universe, do not believe
Those rigid threats of death; ye shall not die:
How should ye? By the fruit? It gives you life
To knowledge. By the threatener? Look on me,
Me who have touched and tasted, yet both live,
And life more perfect have attained than fate
Meant me, by venturing higher than my lot.
Shall that be shut to man, which to the beast
Is open? Or will God incense his ire
For such a petty trespass, and not praise
Rather your dauntless virtue . . .

(IX. 684–94)

With a similar breadth of contrast in expression, Milton may astonish with Eve's delicate love-lyric for Adam:

With thee conversing I forget all time,
All seasons and their change, all please alike.
Sweet is the breath of morn, her rising sweet,
With charm of earliest birds; pleasant the sun
When first on this delightful land he spreads
His orient beams, on herb, tree, fruit, and flower,
Glistering with dew; fragrant the fertile earth
After soft showers; and sweet the coming on
Of grateful evening mild, then silent night

With this her solemn bird and this fair moon,
And these the gems of heaven, her starry train.

(IV. 639–49)

– or with her stinging accusations against Adam, blaming him for the Fall:

Was I to have never parted from thy side?
As good have grown there still a lifeless rib.
Being as I am, why didst not thou the head
Command me absolutely not to go,
Going into such danger as thou saidst?
Too facile then thou didst not much gainsay,
Nay didst permit, approve, and fair dismiss.
Hadst thou been firm and fixed in thy dissent,
Neither had I transgressed, nor thou with me.

(IX. 1153–61)

As a last example of the flexibility and intensity of Milton's poetic use of language, consider these lines from a key moment in the poem. Eve has just returned from eating the forbidden fruit, and Adam, concerned at her delay, has come to meet her with a present of a garland of flowers. She tells him what she has done:

Thus Eve with countenance blithe her story told;
But in her cheek distemper flushing glowed.
On the other side, Adam, soon as he heard
The fatal trespass done by Eve, amazed,
Astonied stood and blank, while horror chill
Ran through his veins, and all his joints relaxed;
From his slack hand the garland wreathed for Eve
Down dropped, and all the faded roses shed:
Speechless he stood and pale, till thus at length
First to himself he inward silence broke.

(IX. 886–95)

This crucial moment is here superbly presented. Eve's 'distemper', or disturbance (even intoxication), is visible as a warm glow on her cheek, and not only qualifies her 'blithe' manner, but is also sharply counterbalanced, through the emphatic placing of 'glowed', by the contrasting 'horror chill' which is similarly placed, three lines later. Then 'amazed,/Astonied stood and blank' enacts Adam's stupefaction by giving emphasis to the three adjectives, at the end of a line, at the beginning of a line (connected by the alliterative 'a' which also connects them to 'Adam' in the previous line), and then in the middle of the line, separated by the verb 'stood', and before a pause. Four lines later, 'speechless he stood and pale' echoes 'astonied stood and blank', thus reinforcing the impression of Adam's horrified consternation. Other inversions in these lines ('down dropped', 'roses shed', 'silence broke') perhaps confirm the transmission of Adam's shock into the world of nature, and highlight his own inner tension: compare Milton's lines above with a translation into a kind of 'everyday' word-order like this:

> *The garland wreathed for Eve from his slack hand*
> *Dropped down and shed all the faded roses:*
> *He stood speechless and pale, till thus at length*
> *He first broke inward silence to himself.*

Though here the alliteration remains, the rhythm is flat or awkward, and Milton's fine two-line movement from 'speechless' to 'silence broke' is ruined. Milton's epic style repeatedly demonstrates its flexibility and a capacity for an intensity of poetic statement that is quite breathtaking. When we read the quoted lines, for instance, we are reminded of how, before this disaster, Adam and Eve 'embracing slept,/And on their naked limbs the flowery roof/Showered roses' (IV. 771–3), an echo which intensifies the poignancy of this moment. A familiarity with the whole poem enriches its individual moments, and impressions of 'difficulty' quite disappear.

An epic poem operates on a grand scale. Milton, like other writers, has idiosyncrasies of style: the addition of an extra adjective after an already qualified noun, for example (as in 'astonied stood and blank', 'speechless he stood and pale', 'th'upright heart and pure', 'sad task and hard' (I. 18; V. 564)) is a technique he derived from Italian poetry, and he uses certain Latin constructions occasionally (as in 'Me of these/Nor skilled nor studious, higher argument/Remains', where the condensed 'me' echoes a Latin dative case (IX. 41–3)). But these idiosyncrasies do not define an epic style. What really is meant, then, by the terms 'epic' and 'epic style'?

Fourteen years after Milton's death, this verse of Dryden's was published in an illustrated edition of *Paradise Lost*:

> *Three poets, in three distant ages born,*
> *Greece, Italy, and England did adorn.*
> *The first in loftiness of thought surpassed,*
> *The next in majesty, in both the last:*

The force of Nature could no farther go;
To make a third, she joined the former two.

The poets which Dryden refers to were the great names associated with epic – Homer, Virgil, and, of course, Milton – and though his praise is in part a conventional encomium, the concepts of 'loftiness' and 'majesty' do suggest some of the qualities associated with epic verse. The grandeur of epic is its essence, since it is a form of large-scale verse which attempts to identify some enduring significance and nobility in human action, to rescue something worthy and admirable from the enclosing darkness of history. In order to be more specific, we may make a distinction in both style and content between epic verse which was composed to be spoken and heard, such as that of Homer, and that which was composed in writing to be read, such as that of Virgil.

'Oral' epic, such as Homer's *Iliad* and *Odyssey*, has a generally less closely integrated and more episodic construction, and tends to use an elegantly archaic language with many stock phrases and repeated epithets. Its central concern is with the prowess and fame of an individual hero, with 'honour' and 'glory', and with personal physical attributes, rather than with the more socialized concerns of 'morality', or collective values. It is the poetry of a comparatively undeveloped society. On the other hand, 'written' epic, such as Virgil's *Aeneid* (and, we might add, Camoes' *Os Lusiadas*, a Portuguese poem published in 1572, but probably known to Milton through an English translation published in 1655, and Tasso's *Gerusalemme Liberata*, an Italian poem published in 1575 and well known to Milton), has generally a denser verbal texture and a more carefully integrated construction, and relies on a more intricate and suggestive choice of words. Of greater importance, perhaps, 'written' epic, arising from more organized and developed societies, celebrates not so much individual qualities, such as strength or courage, but a social ideal: moral strength in one form or another. Virgil's *Aeneid*, for example, though the main action of the poem takes place some three hundred years before the foundation of Rome, and though Aeneas himself is a Trojan, not a Roman, is really concerned with defining, through the story of the Trojan ancestors of Rome, the essence of what it is to be a Roman in the present. Virgil links Aeneas with his own patron and ruler, Augustus, and defines the Roman conception of life and values in a comprehensive vision which combines legend, history, philosophy and religion, and transcends the story of Troy as told by Homer. The poem is didactic, and looks back with a resigned sadness, contrasting the old-type hero, Turnus, whose love of battle and glory proves destructive, with the new hero Aeneas, whose essential quality is his devotion to his duty, or his *pietas*, the embodiment of the desirable Roman social values.

Milton's *Paradise Lost* is a 'written' epic in the tradition of Virgil, but Milton intended that his poem, while resembling its predecessors in manner, should surpass them in certain respects. He includes some traditional epic features, such as accounts of dangerous journeys, personal combat and war, descriptions of gardens and marvellous buildings, scenes in heaven and hell, and visions of the future. (He also excludes other features inappropriate to epic, such as broad comedy, or the celebration of sensual indulgence.) Further, as in other 'written' epics, there is a sense in *Paradise Lost* of a melancholy looking-back: Virgil's *Aeneid* came at the end of the bellicose Caesarean age; Camoes' *Os Lusiados* came at the end of the great period of Portuguese imperialism; and Tasso's *Gerusalemme Liberata*, written at the enlightened court of Ferrara, can be seen as a last great work of the Renaissance spirit. So Milton's *Paradise Lost*, with its melancholy title, can be seen as the epic of English Puritanism, coming at a time when it seemed that the project to create an English theocracy under the guidance of Cromwell had failed. In his poetic examination of the reasons for this failure, Milton chose for his theme not a celebration of secular values, as manifest in the foundation of Rome, or the liberation of Jerusalem, for example, but an analysis of the whole purpose of human life in relation to 'eternal providence' (I. 25). Milton compares his task with that of Homer and Virgil – to their disadvantage:

> *. . . sad task, yet argument*
> *Not less but more heroic than the wrath*
> *Of stern Achilles on his foe pursued*
> *Thrice fugitive about Troy wall; or rage*
> *Of Turnus for Lavinia disespoused.*
>
> (IX. 13–17)

Milton rejects the Homeric heroism, which is described by Michael in the poem as part of man's degeneration after the Fall – 'For in those days might only shall be admired,/And valour and heroic virtue called' (XI. 689–90) – as he rejects the empty descriptions of the heroic in 'battles feigned', preferring a 'higher argument' which involves the 'better fortitude/Of patience and heroic martyrdom' (IX. 29–32, 42). The subject may attract 'fit audience, . . . though few', but the inspiration he claims is the spirit of God, truth itself, in contrast with the 'empty dream' of the muses of previous epic poets (VII. 31, 39).

For such a grand task, therefore, no less than the patiently heroic struggle of good and bad in human souls, Milton needed and created a grand style, capable of sustained impressiveness, yet also flexible and subtle. The sense, as Milton wrote in his note on the verse which justifies the absence of rhyme, is 'variously drawn out from one verse [i.e. 'line'] into another', and by overflowing the individual lines the style achieves a powerful and unique fullness of statement. The experience of countless readers over three centuries is that familiarity with the flow of Milton's verse makes it compulsive. This study, however, is designed to illuminate the poem through an attempt to understand the problems and issues it addresses, as well as to identify its poetic felicities. The poem is 'about' both seventeenth-century politics and biblical history, 'about' both how the world can be explained and how to live as an individual in it. Milton's *Paradise Lost* was intended to be, in a sense, the 'ultimate' epic: if we respond to its problems and failures as well as to its achievements and successes, the poem's meaning for us will be significantly enhanced.

2 Time in the Poem

The action of the poem happens during five days, with a week's gap between the third and fourth days:

DAY ONE: The events of Books I and II, from the awakening of Satan and the rebel angels in hell, through the building of Pandaemonium and the council meeting, to Satan's departure from hell and journey through chaos.

DAY TWO: The events of Books III and IV, from Satan's arrival on the universe at about midnight, Paradise-time (he is described as being both directly above Paradise and in 'night's extended shade', i.e. on the other side of earth from the sun (III. 527, 557)), through his conversation on the sun with Uriel 'at highth of noon' (IV. 564), to his expulsion from Paradise by Gabriel at or near midnight (IV. 1015).

DAY THREE: The events of the *main action* in Books V to VIII, from sunrise, when Adam wakes up (V. 1–3), through noon, when Raphael arrives (V. 311), and the extended conversation with Adam, to sunset, when Raphael leaves (VIII. 630).

(*Seven days elapse while Satan circles the earth in darkness, on the other side from the sun* (*IX. 62–7*))

DAY FOUR: The events of Books IX and X, from Satan's re-entry to Paradise at midnight (IX. 58), through the Fall, about noon (IX. 739), the Messiah's judgment of mankind in early evening (X. 92–5), the exit and return of Satan to Paradise and his return to hell (X. 339–42), the arrival of Sin and Death in Paradise (X. 585–6), to Adam's remorse, during which he refers to the Messiah's judgment as 'this day' and later as 'that day' (X. 773, 1050).

DAY FIVE: The events of the *main action* in Books XI and XII, from sunrise and the arrival of Michael (XI. 173), through the preview of history, to the eviction of Adam and Eve from Paradise at 'the hour precise', twenty-four hours after the Fall (XII. 589).

This is the main action of the poem. In addition there are two secondary stories: Raphael tells Adam of events before the main action, relating to the War in Heaven and the creation of the universe (Books V to VIII), and Michael reveals to Adam events to come afterwards, from Cain's murder of Abel to the Last Judgment (Books XI and XII). We can therefore construct a chronology prior to the events of the main action, which will allow us to account for twenty-two days immediately before the opening of the poem:

1. ONE DAY: The Exaltation of Christ, which sets off the rebellion of Satan, and therefore the rest of the action (V. 603, 618).

2. THREE DAYS: The War in Heaven, which starts the day after the Exaltation and lasts for three days (V. 642; VI. 748).

3. NINE DAYS: The pursuit of the defeated rebel angels from heaven to hell (VI. 871).

4. NINE MORE DAYS: The rebel angels lie stupefied in hell before Satan awakes and starts the main action of the poem (I. 50).

In addition, during this period the creation of the universe, including that of Adam and Eve, occurs. The creation takes place after the Son returns from the pursuit of the rebel angels to hell (VII. 131–64), and, as in the Bible, it takes six days. For the account of the creation, Milton uses the biblical 'day' which comprises 'even and morn', and goes therefore from 6 p.m. to 6 p.m.: thus the 'seventh evening' comes immediately at the end of the sixth day, when Adam and Eve were created (VII. 550, 581–2).

If the creation begins immediately on the return of the Son from the pursuit of the rebel angels to hell, then it starts on day fourteen, and Adam and Eve are created on day nineteen (i.e. the sixth day of creation), three days before the opening of the main action of the poem. Alternatively, the poem allows a different possibility. Raphael tells Adam that he was absent from heaven on the day that Adam was created, on an 'excursion toward the gates of hell', and that he heard from within the sound of 'torment and loud lament and furious rage' (VIII.231, 244). Since Satan's first speech breaks the 'horrid silence' of hell, and the rebels were until then in a stupor on the lake of fire, the noise heard by Raphael could well be that of their rage after Satan has aroused them (I. 83, 280, 666). In this case, the creation of Adam and Eve must take place three days later, on day twenty-two, the very day on which the poem opens with Satan's awakening in hell. Either interpretation is legitimate, though the latter has a certain dramatic appropriateness, with the creation of mankind taking place as the 'hidden story' while Satan and the rebels are planning their strategies in hell. (The main argument against this view is the phraseology which sometimes implies that Adam has been around for some time, e.g. at IV. 449 and V. 3, 31.) In either case, however, the six days of creation must take place during the nine days' stupor of the rebel angels in hell.

3 Place in the Poem

There are five distinct locations for the action of the poem:

1. HEAVEN. Heaven is a 'city' with gates and battlements where the angels live and God has his throne (though the word is also used in the poem to describe the space above the earth and under the stars, i.e. within the universe, as in VII. 232). Milton is prepared to admit doubt as to the shape of heaven ('undetermined square or round'), though Sin in the poem refers to it as a 'quadrature', implying squareness, compared with the 'orbicular', or round, universe (II. 1048; X. 381).

2. CHAOS. Chaos is the name of what we might call 'outer space', and is 'a dark,/Illimitable ocean without bound' (II. 891–2). It is filled with uncreated matter, where there is 'eternal anarchy, amidst the noise/Of endless wars', as unordered 'atoms' struggle with each other (II. 896–900). Creation, whether of hell or of the universe, uses the raw material and territory of Chaos (II. 999–1006). Satan has a difficult journey through Chaos to get from hell to the universe, though it is made much easier after the Fall when Sin and Death build a bridge, which he uses on his return to hell.

3. HELL. Milton's hell is not under the earth, as in some medieval cosmographies, but is an enclosed and fiery 'concave' at the outermost limits of chaos, the gates of which are guarded by Sin and Death (II. 635, 1003). It is a place of varied geography, including plains, hills, and valleys, as well as the location of the magnificent palace of Pandaemonium

(I. 756). Its distinctive characteristic is that it is a place of 'fierce extremes', including a 'burning lake' and a 'frozen continent' (I. 210; II. 587, 599). Its inhabitants are the rebel angels, and it was created in anticipation of their rebellion as a result of God's foreknowledge (I. 70–71).

4. THE 'WORLD'. When Milton uses the word 'world', he normally means what we would call 'universe'. Though Raphael does speculate 'what if the sun/Be centre to the world', the universe of the poem is earth-centred (VIII. 122–3). Such a conception of the universe clearly has philosophical implications for the importance of mankind in God's plans, and therefore Milton presumably felt justified in rejecting (though offering for consideration) the Copernican sun-centred theory, first published more than a century earlier, in 1543. Also, while Galileo is the only near-contemporary figure referred to by name in the poem, Milton is not persuaded to accept his support for the Copernican thesis which had been published in 1610 (V. 262; also I. 288). The creation of the 'world' is described as the result of 'enclosing' it from Chaos (III.420–21; VII.218–232). When Satan journeys from hell to earth, he first lands on the 'firm opacous [i.e. 'opaque'] globe' of the outside of the 'world', or universe (III. 418). Since he is above the 'starry sphere', the only illumination is from the 'wall of heaven' (III. 416, 427). The 'world' hangs from heaven by a golden chain, and there is both a ladder up to heaven, and a passage down to earth at the centre of the 'world' (II. 1051; III. 523–8). Later, Sin and Death build a large bridge from hell to the point on the outside of the 'world' on which Satan first landed (X. 315–18).

5. EARTH. On earth, Eden is the name of the land in which Paradise is located, 'the happy seat of man' (III. 632). Paradise is an elevated spot surrounded by a 'steep wilderness', and has walls and only one gate, to the east (IV. 135, 178).

The action of the poem moves between all these locations, though inevitably, from Book IV onwards, concentrating on Paradise. The various journeys between them by, in particular, Satan emphasize the vastness of Milton's symbolic universe, which is entirely appropriate to the vastness of his subject-matter, which attempts to give a comprehensive historical, religious, and moral framework for human life, centred on the concept of losing paradise.

4 Losing Paradise

One striking feature of 'paradise' as an idea is that it is always being lost. In fact, we may conclude that its extraordinary tendency to be gone is its most significant feature. It is always somewhere else, remote in space or time or imagination, like eighteenth-century Tahiti, or the biblical Garden of Eden, or our own childhood. What is the effect of this common invocation of an irretrievable paradise? By contrast with our everyday life it might serve to make us feel limited and dissatisfied, bounded as we are by the unalterable factors of our own history and biology. As a result, the loss of a supposed paradise can be used both to describe our present position in an imperfect world and to produce guidelines for behaviour which might get it back. Paradise thus becomes a moral sanction: 'you lost it because you were bad, but you might get it back if you are good in future'. This is precisely the promise made to Adam at the end of *Paradise Lost*: 'then wilt thou not be loath/To leave this Paradise, but shalt possess/A paradise within thee, happier far' (XII. 585–7).

A second problem with paradise is that on close analysis it is very difficult to define: it just keeps slipping away. For example, this world of ours can be felt as a world of unending struggle, both for survival in the natural world and for position or affluence in the social world. So let us create our imagined paradise as a world without struggle, where survival is guaranteed and where all social positions are fixed. But then we find we are not 'free', particularly if a condition of membership is unquestioning obedience to the royal family. Contemplating such a world, we might even come to believe that some of the finest human achievements are those made in the struggle against adversity. Expressed as a paradox, this is to say that knowledge of good comes only through knowledge of evil, and this perception is the foundation of the ancient Christian doctrine of the 'Fortunate Fall', which claims that the loss of paradise (or, the 'Fall') was, in certain respects, a good thing for the human race. This doctrine Milton accepts as the basis of the argument of *Paradise Lost*.[1]

The poem concerns itself with the loss of two paradises: one is Adam and Eve's loss of Paradise in Eden, and the other is Satan's loss of heaven. The biblical authority for the story of the eviction of the human pair from their Paradise in Eden is the third chapter of Genesis, whereas for the story of the War in Heaven it is basically just three verses (7–9) in Revelation, chapter 12. On the face of it, then, Milton's emphasis on Satan's story, which dominates the opening books, is quite remarkable. Dryden observed that 'the devil' was Milton's hero 'instead of Adam' (though it should be noted that this is not the same point as that made by Blake a century later when he wrote approvingly that Milton was 'of the Devil's party without knowing it', or by Shelley who wrote that 'Milton's Devil as a moral being is . . . far superior to his God').[2] Dryden's observation reminds us that in the poem the Fall of Eve and then Adam is secondary to that of Satan, and induced by him.

Milton had abandoned an idea some years earlier, in 1642, of writing a tragedy on the subject *Adam Unparadised.* To write an epic rather than a tragedy, however, required grand action which only the story of Satan could provide in this context. But the emphasis on Satan's story also allowed Milton the scope to raise two fundamental questions which Adam and Eve's story in itself could not raise so directly. These are questions of power and identity: one is 'Is God omnipotent?', and the other is 'Am I autonomous like God, or was I created?' They are fundamental questions because, in one form or another, everyone has to answer them. It is not necessary to believe in God in a religious sense to need to ask whether there is an ultimate omnipotent force that makes the historical and social world as it is rather than otherwise, on the analogy perhaps of the atomic and electromagnetic forces in the natural world. In fact, when Blake wrote that 'in Milton, the Father is Destiny', he was acknowledging that the religious terminology of 'God the Father' is only another way of addressing the secular concept of 'Destiny'; likewise Milton's own words, 'God and nature bid the same', recognize the same idea (VI. 176).[3] Satan and his angels can only find out whether God is omnipotent by rebellion and resistance, but even then no clear answer emerges. They are doomed to struggle, and so the Big Debate in Pandaemonium is about what form that struggle should take. The second question addresses that illusion of independence which we create for ourselves, both individually and collectively. To assert autonomy is to deny our brotherhood and sisterhood, to deny the shared values which have been historically produced and which form the nucleus of our identity. It is to regard everything outside ourselves as material for our exploitation. Satan is hypnotized by this possibility: 'Better to reign in hell, than serve in heaven', he exclaims (I. 263). Satan needs to believe in his autonomy for his self-justification: it is only when approaching Paradise at the start of Book IV that, in William Empson's phrase, 'his nerve breaks', and in his first soliloquy he acknowledges his created status (IV. 43).[4] Thereafter he degenerates rapidly from the heroic figure of the opening books.

5 Providence

Milton's explicit objective in writing *Paradise Lost* was to conduct a 'great argument' in order to 'assert eternal providence,/And justify the ways of God to men' (I. 24–6). Although the poem has religious concerns, it is not a religious poem in the sense of a work which inspires religious devotion. There is nothing in the poem which suggests any warmth about the person of Christ, for example. The poet's statement of intent to 'assert' and 'justify', activities of the head rather than of the heart, are more appropriate in a legal or secular rather than a religious context. What the poet is claiming as his task is to demonstrate the ultimate justice of God, and thus to prove the existence of Providence – that is, to prove that the world is not governed by blind chance, but that events have meaning and purpose. There are special reasons why Milton might have felt the necessity for doing this in particular in the late 1650s and early 1660s, when the poem was written.

For the previous twenty years, during his thirties and forties, Milton had devoted his energies to the reform of Church and society in England, largely through the publication of controversial pamphlets. From 1629, the year in which Milton had graduated from Christ's College, Cambridge, with a B.A. degree, until 1640, a few months after Milton had returned from a fifteen-month continental tour spent mainly in Italy, Charles I had ruled England without a parliament. One of his chief advisers had been William Laud, the bad-tempered little Archbishop of Canterbury, who had become notorious for attempting to impose high-church ways upon the reformed national church, mainly in order to claim continuity with the pre-Reformation church. While in Italy, Milton had met the then pathetic figure of Galileo, as he put it, 'grown old a prisoner to the Inquisition, for thinking in astronomy otherwise than the Franciscan and Dominican licensers thought'.[5] In 1639, just before Milton's return from Italy, Charles had taken an army of 20,000 in order to suppress the Scottish Covenanters, who had risen to resist the forced introduction of bishops (as opposed to presbyters, or elders) into their Church, along with the English liturgy. A peace treaty led to the establishment of a General Assembly for the settlement of civil and religious grievances in Scotland, which promptly abolished episcopacy (the bishops) there. In this political and religious context Milton returned to England from Italy, strenuously determined to defend the ancient liberties of the English people, for which, in authoritarian Catholic Italy, the English were renowned. In 1641 and 1642 he wrote five vitriolic pamphlets against episcopacy: the bishops, Milton claimed, 'though they had renounc'd the *Pope*, they still hugg'd the *Popedome* ... persecuting the *Protestants* no slacker then the Pope would have done'.[6] Within four years episcopacy was abolished in England and, incidentally, Laud had been executed. As Milton himself wrote, reflecting on this period some eight years later in 1654:

> When the bishops, at whom every man aimed his arrow, had at length fallen, and we were now at leisure, as far as they were concerned, I began to turn my thoughts to other subjects; to consider in what way I could contribute to the

progress of real and substantial liberty; which is to be sought for not from without, but within, and is to be obtained principally not by fighting, but by the just regulation and by the proper conduct of life.[7]

The need for private, internal reformation becomes later a major theme of *Paradise Lost*, but 1642 became a time for fighting, as civil war broke out following the resistance of parliament (which had been recalled in 1640) to Charles I's arbitrary rule. In 1644, the year of the first decisive battle of the war when Cromwell defeated the royalist troops at Marston Moor, Milton published one of his most famous pamphlets, *Areopagitica*. It attacks a parliamentary decision of the previous year to restrict the freedom of the press, and recalls both the Italian journey and the anti-episcopal arguments:

That freedom of writing should be restrained by a discipline imitated from the Prelats, and learnt by them from the Inquisition to shut us up all again into the breast of a licencer, must needs give cause of doubt and discouragement to all learned and religious men.[8]

At this time also, between 1643 and 1645, Milton published four pamphlets which became notorious among his enemies and which advocated a liberalization of the divorce laws, essentially again in the interest of promoting liberty – though not licence – against custom, 'according to the divine law which Christ has never abrogated', for, he argued, 'it is to little purpose for him to make a noise about liberty in the legislative assemblies, and in the courts of justice, who is in bondage to an inferior at home'.[9] In 1649 Charles was executed, and within two weeks Milton published an eloquent pamphlet, *The Tenure of Kings and Magistrates*, which justifies the execution of a king who breaches the trust put in him by the people, and attacks with scorn the shallow opportunism and weakness of the Presbyterians, who by this time were, by and large, against the execution and in favour of a 'moderate' settlement. 'New Presbyter is but Old Priest writ large', he wrote in a poem at the time.[10] Soon afterwards it was the Independents in the army, representing that other diverse branch of the puritan tradition, with Cromwell at their head, who gained the upper hand over the Presbyterians. Shortly after the proclamation of the Commonwealth in 1649, Milton was appointed Secretary of Foreign Tongues to the Council of State – a crucially important diplomatic post in what we would call the Foreign Office – and he published two further defences of the Commonwealth within the next five years. He held his diplomatic post for over ten years, even though by 1652 he had probably become totally blind, possibly as a result of a tumour of the pituitary gland. He probably began serious work on

Paradise Lost in about 1658, and continued working on it until it was finished in its first form in about 1663, after the Restoration of the monarchy which took place in 1660.

How are we to interpret and understand these tumultuous years, and in particular the effect they may have had on Milton's view of the working of Providence? Was not the hand of Providence to be seen, using the scholar and poet John Milton as its instrument, cleansing the English nation of false religious practices and of an unworthy king, and instituting instead a free commonwealth of citizens under God? Milton held firmly to the belief that the English were God's chosen nation because an Englishman, John Wycliffe (1320?–84), had begun the Reformation in England. In his famous address to Parliament in 1644, Milton had asked:

> Why else was this Nation chos'n before any other, that out of her as out of *Sion* should be proclaim'd and sounded forth the first tidings and trumpet of Reformation of all *Europ*. And had it not bin the obstinat perversnes of our Prelats against the divine and admirable spirit of *Wicklef*, to suppresse him as a schismatic and *innovator* ... the glory of reforming all our neighbours had bin compleatly ours.[11]

The evidence that John Milton had inherited the mantle of John Wycliffe, as part of the long-term workings of Providence, seemed unmistakable at the time. But then it all went wrong. 'The disunity of the radicals, the ambitions of the generals, the self-interested a-politicism of the mass of middle-class Englishmen, had defeated the hopes of Milton and his kind for creating a good society in England', comments Christopher Hill.[12] By 1657 Cromwell had become king in all but name, and in 1660 the old monarchy was restored. Milton remained consistent in his views during these years: he was opposed to rule by any single person, whether a Charles or a Cromwell, and in fearless defiance of any self-interest he published his last major pamphlet, *The Readie and Easie Way to Establish a Free Commonwealth*, on the eve of the Restoration in 1660. In it he quotes the example of the Israelites who demanded a king:

> They had thir longing; but with this testimonie of God's wrath; *ye shall cry out in that day because of your king whom ye shall have chosen, and the Lord will not hear you in that day* (I Samuel 8:18). Us if he shall hear now, how much less will he hear when we cry heerafter, who once deliverd by him from a king, and not without wondrous acts of his providence, insensible and unworthie of those high mercies, are returning precipitantly, if he withhold us not, back to the captivitie from whence he freed us.[13]

Milton was imprisoned later in the year.

So why had God apparently abandoned his chosen people? Both episcopacy and monarchy were now re-established, and Milton was blind and in public disgrace. Who was to blame for the deterioration of Commonwealth ideals? Had Milton proved inadequate, and been struck blind as a punishment? Had the English people failed their God? Or had God failed his people? This last was the unthinkable. Perhaps Milton's feelings at this time are an echo of the lines he gave Samson in his dramatic poem *Samson Agonistes*. The Israelites have not been freed from Philistine rule, and Samson himself, their one-time hope for deliverance, is blind and in slavery to the Philistines:

> *Promise was that I*
> *Should Israel from Philistian yoke deliver;*
> *Ask for this great deliverer now, and find him*
> *Eyeless in Gaza at the mill with slaves,*
> *Himself in bonds under Philistian yoke;*
> *Yet stay, let me not rashly call in doubt*
> *Divine prediction; what if all foretold*
> *Had been fulfilled but through mine own default,*
> *Whom have I to complain of but myself?*
>
> (38–46)

Just as Samson later, in a supreme act of selfless courage, pulled down the Philistine theatre in atonement for his 'own default', so Milton set out to deploy his strength, in a supreme effort of epic composition, to assert eternal providence and justify the ways of God. He chose the grandest story of all time: the first rebellions in heaven and earth.

Protestants since at least the sixteenth century had believed that daily happenings were signs of God's intervention, and they saw in personal and public events a *pattern* which apparently indicated divine control. This belief was in denial of the heathen concept of an arbitrary 'fate' or 'fortune', because of the necessary involvement of people's own moral behaviour, individually or collectively, in their success or failure, happiness or disaster. Occurrences, both trivial and important, could be seen as omens for the future, or as punishment or reward for past deeds. Even Archbishop Laud is reported to have been profoundly shaken to find, one day in 1640, that his portrait on his study wall had fallen to the floor.[14] John Foxe, in his *Book of Martyrs*, as it became known, first published in 1563, had popularized the myth that the English were a people chosen by God, and thereafter it became a powerful element in Protestant preaching that England's 'lucky escapes', such as from the Armada (1588), or from the Gunpowder Plot (1605), were manifestations of God's hand, and that the fortunes of English kings varied according to the godliness of their behaviour and policies. The puritan obligation to record personal evidence of God's 'providences' led to the vogue for diaries and autobiographies in the seventeenth century, in which coincidences (as they might be called today) were noted for their moral significance. In the late 1650s a project was even initiated by the Presbyterian minister Matthew Poole for the collection, county by county, of 'illustrious Providences', in order that a complete list might be compiled, in a manner analogous to the new scientific method for collecting and classifying natural phenomena.

Providences, however, are not as easy to collect and classify as birds or insects. An event often cited by Protestants during the seventeenth century as evidence of God's judgment was the death or injury in October 1623 of nearly a hundred Roman Catholics in a church in Blackfriars, London, when the floor collapsed. The Catholics, however, saw the event as merely the unfortunate result of rotten floorboards. It was, therefore, inevitably problematic to explain history in 'providential' terms, since, side by side with this language of providence, the language of 'natural' explanation developed. Yet it nevertheless seemed that the assertion of God's ultimate sovereignty as manifested in providences was the last safeguard against a world of moral chaos, however inscrutable the workings of providence might seem to the untutored or cynical eye. The concept of providence did at least instil a strong sense of personal responsibility in people, and was an idea useful in the upbringing of children, and thus was a central tenet of Protestant individualism. *Paradise Lost*, in asserting 'eternal Providence', thus attempts to uncover the hidden pattern of history in the context of a moral universe under God's direction. Perhaps the events of the 1640s and 1650s were leading to a moral lesson which was as yet not fully understood: the lesson of patience, of humility, and of individual struggle.

For Milton, the stories of the Fall of Satan and the angels, the War in Heaven, and the Fall of Adam and Eve were at the same time *historical* events and *symbolic* events. As symbolic events they prefigured man's propensity for establishing ideals and failing to live up to them. The failure of the English Revolution thus may be seen as a re-enactment of an archetypal historical pattern. From this perspective a narrative about supernatural and prehistoric events, as in *Paradise Lost*, can be seen to have relevance to events in history: in a sense such a narrative contains the history of the world by prefiguring its possibilities. How this sense of a contained, 'cyclical' view of history came to be replaced by the 'linear' view which in general we assume today (according to which change occurs in a *developmental* way, often associated with some notion of 'progress', rather than in a *repetitive* way) has been called by the historian Keith Thomas 'one of the great mysteries of intellectual history'.[15] He suggests that perhaps a *sense* of irrevocable change is only produced by the *fact* of technological change, and, in particular in the sixteenth and seventeenth centuries, it was the effects of gunpowder, the printing press, and the mariner's compass which reminded people that they could never recapture the ancient world.

Paradise Lost is caught exactly at that moment of crucial shift from one view of history to another: Milton chooses the oldest of literary forms, the epic, just at the time when the foundations of our modern secular world were being laid, through the growing ascendancy of the middle classes and the accompanying explosion of technological and capitalist enterprise. In the note at the beginning of the poem which explains his rejection of rhyme, Milton claims both to be innovative, and to be recovering 'ancient liberty', when he defends his neglect of rhyme as 'an example set, the first in English, of ancient liberty recovered to heroic poem from the troublesome and modern bondage of rhyming', and his muse is soon invoked to pursue 'things unattempted yet in prose or rhyme' (I. 16). It was the last moment in our history when a poem on such a grand religious theme could be conceived as having direct contemporary relevance.

Having noticed the context in which the composition of *Paradise Lost* took place, however, we must be careful not to misunderstand the reader's task of interpretation. All reading involves interpretation, whether this is a self-conscious act or not, and it is the literary conventions in a work which guide us in establishing meanings. But the epic and religious conventions at work in *Paradise Lost* do not make the poem an *allegory*, that is, do not make the poem a story with a hidden 'true' story which may be uncovered by a simple act of identifying correspondences. We would not only be wrong to say that Satan 'is' Cromwell (the rebel) or Charles I (the tyrant) or even Milton (the scourge of autocracy), but even to pose the question 'Who is Satan *really*?' would produce only an inadequate answer and a gross limitation of the significance of the poem. Milton's method is *allusive* rather than allegorical, and while alluding to aspects of Cromwell, or Charles I, or Milton himself in Satan, the portrayal of Satan in the poem is more than the sum of these references or allusions. Satan doubtless includes these (and other) allusions, but is as multifarious as the language in which he is embodied, and as varied as, for example, the nature of hell itself in the poem. But, on the other hand, Satan is not merely a supernatural character in an improbable drama: he manifestly does embody allusions to human affairs. When, in Book V, Raphael is chatting at Adam and Eve's lunch-party, and is about to give an account of recent events in heaven, he says:

> *... what surmounts the reach*
> *Of human sense, I shall delineate so,*
> *By likening spiritual to corporal forms,*
> *As may express them best, though what if earth*
> *Be but the shadow of heaven, and things therein*
> *Each to other like, more than on earth is thought?*
>
> (V. 571–6)

It may be useful to think of Satan in this light partly as representative of the public world of politics and rebellion, and his presentation as an exploration of the ambitions and failures, the egotism and despair, that public life offers. In this his role is therefore complemented in the poem by the private, domestic world of Adam and Eve, in whose interpersonal relations are enacted the possibilities and problems of freedom and self-restraint, of desire and failure.

II The First Day: Hell, and Satan's Journey

1 Inspiration: I. 1–26

The first six lines of the poem outline its whole action: 'disobedience ... fruit ... taste... death... restore ... regain'. The words 'fruit' and 'taste' are central to the imagery of *Paradise Lost*, and, together with 'woe', recur repeatedly through the poem. Here, at the ends of the first lines, they receive their initial emphasis. Equally important is the idea of restoring and regaining what was lost by disobedience. The explanation of why and how this will happen is what will, according to Milton's intention, 'justify the ways of God to men' (I. 26). (Feminists must accept the male-oriented language as part of the heritage of protestantism, though gender-relations later in the poem become one of its interesting issues.) The project of explaining the hidden meaning of history is undertaken by Milton through a claim to 'inspiration', which is in essence a claim to authority.

But Milton's 'muse', which provides the inspiration, is rather cryptic. There are four invocations of the muse in the poem, at the beginnings of Books I, III, VII and IX. In this first book the muse is clearly the Holy Spirit, although Milton elsewhere argues that there is no biblical precedent for invoking the Holy Spirit.[1] This muse 'dove-like sat'st brooding on the vast abyss/And madest it pregnant' – an allusion to the ancient doctrine that God is both feminine ('brooding') and masculine ('madest ... pregnant'). It was thus the Spirit which both created the universe and which inspired Moses, the first person to tell the story of Paradise Lost, to whom Milton felt himself successor. In Book VII, however, he suggests the muse might be called Urania, a non-biblical name, and in Book IX he refers to her almost as his unconscious: 'celestial patroness, who deigns/Her nightly visitation unimplored,/And dictates to me slumbering, or inspires/Easy my unpremeditated verse' (VII. 1; IX. 21–4). Here in Book I he states his intention that his words will 'soar/Above the Aonian mount', which is a way of asserting the superiority of his inspiration to that previously provided by mere pagan muses in earlier epics, the Aonian mount, or Helicon, being their legendary sanctuary. It was common in the seventeenth century for classical myths to be considered as distorted versions, or echoes, of biblical episodes. For example, the first book of Ovid's *Metamorphoses* contains a story of an earth-wide flood which is in many ways similar to the story of Noah in Genesis, chapters 6–8, though Ovid's hero, who survives with his wife on a boat, is called Deucalion. This belief made it possible for the Christian to respect classical myths, and to find in them 'human' truths, while at the same time recognizing their historical untruth. Thus Milton in *Paradise Lost* makes reference to both classical and biblical sources.

By 1667, however, the year of the first publication of *Paradise Lost*, the idea of 'inspiration', together with its correlative 'enthusiasm', was coming to be considered dangerous. It was associated in establishment minds with the turbulence of the recent Civil War period, when the notion of direct inspiration from God had seemed to justify radicalism and subversion, both religious and political. The year 1667 also saw the publication of *The History of the Royal Society of London*, by Thomas Sprat, in which he defines the first purpose of the Society as 'the satisfaction of breathing a freer air, and of conversing in quiet, one with another, without being engag'd in the passions and madness of that dismal age', together with the raising of young men 'invincibly arm'd against all the enchantments of enthusiasm [i.e. 'religious radicalism']'. Sprat also argues for the Society's linguistic style, which is 'a constant resolution to reject all amplifications, digressions, and swellings of style; to return back to the primitive purity and shortness, when men deliver'd so many things almost in an equal number of words'.[2] Milton's inspiration is not the passionate expression of private emotion: that romantic idea did not arrive on the literary scene for another century. In fact, Milton would have had some sympathy with Sprat's rejection of 'passions and madness', for in *Paradise Lost* this is the clue to Milton's justification of the ways of God to men. The inspired poem defines the nature of the Fall not just as 'disobedience' in itself, nor even as the desire for forbidden knowledge and power in themselves, but as the domination of passion over reason. Since reason liberates and passion enslaves, and since, for Milton, 'God and Nature bid the same', disobedience to the bidding of God and Nature is not only unnatural, but also irrational and enslaving. *Paradise Lost* attempts to show the way to individual and collective liberation by a defence of reason, but it is not the cold experimentalism of Charles II's Royal Society that Milton advocates. The poem is, in fact, deeply against its age: as Milton writes in the invocation to Book VII, 'I sing ... unchanged/... though fallen on evil days' (VII. 24–5). The poem rejects, in its style, not only the 'modern bondage of rhyming', but also the easy seductions of poetic passion and any simplified attempt to identify words and things as advocated by Sprat.[3] The verse is in parts tough, but also subtle and exciting; above all it does not submit to the cosy pieties and political compromises of Restoration England. It celebrates the rational process of individual self-analysis and, where appropriate, of resistance.

2 Satan and Hell's Angels: I. 27–669

The muse, when asked the Big Question, 'What cause/Moved our ... parents ... to fall off/From their creator?', answers unambiguously: 'The infernal serpent' (I. 34). The explanation of man's first disobedience, then, involves a prior story – that of Satan, who is identified with the serpent in Revelation 12:9, and in particular it concerns the story of his aspiration 'to set himself in glory' and 'to have equalled the most high' (I. 39–40). The aspiration leads to the War in Heaven, details of which are recounted later in the poem in Book VI, but at this point all that concerns us immediately is the result:

> *He ... with ambitious aim*
> *Against the throne and monarchy of God*
> *Raised impious war in heaven and battle proud*
> *With vain attempt. Him the almighty power*
> *Hurled headlong flaming from the ethereal sky*
> *With hideous ruin and combustion down*
> *To bottomless perdition, there to dwell*
> *In adamantine chains and penal fire,*
> *Who durst defy the omnipotent to arms.*
>
> (I. 41–9)

The oppositional awkwardness of the words on the war are here followed by the great alliterative flood of the casting-out, where the inversion of the normal word-order ('Him the almighty power/Hurled') is sensed momentarily to be an absolutely appropriate enactment of the sense, particularly if the reader does not pause for breath before 'perdition'. Here also the first use in the poem of the words 'almighty' and 'omnipotent' in the authoritative epic voice of the poet gives us information which Satan at this point either does not know or cannot accept. He is now, with his followers, cast into a new environment characterized by fire. Satan later tells us that 'my self am hell' (IV. 75), so we should see this new location as that condition of the human heart where

> *... darkness visible*
> *Served only to discover sights of woe,*
> *Regions of sorrow, doleful shades, where peace*
> *And rest can never dwell, hope never comes*

> *That comes to all; but torture without end*
> *Still urges . . .*
>
> (I. 63–8)

The paradox of 'darkness visible' is no paradox if we understand it to portray that consciousness of self that is the distinctive characteristic of human life. The *awareness that he is aware* of his 'darkness' is what makes the darkness visible to Satan, and intensifies the sorrow and loss of peace, rest, and hope. His self-awareness is the torment, and, like any political or military leader, Satan must produce a persona, or public face, in order to 'save face', in the first two books of the poem.

The discrepancy between public image and private thoughts becomes most clear when the heroic figure of the opening books first soliloquizes in Book IV. What the fall of Satan has produced is that distressing and endless complexity of ambition, failure, private self-reproach, desperation, action, failure, etc., which leaves him and his followers unstable and vacillating in that neurotic zone between genuine aspiration and destructive (and self-destructive) anger, cheered only by their stirring rhetoric. But Satan's challenging of omnipotence is only a 'crime' (I. 79) because we wish to imagine history, or 'life', without opposition, rebellion or struggle. This imaginary history of perfect peace, harmony, and happiness is actually no real history, because such a time has never existed, but it is rather a denial of history, and we call it 'heaven', or 'paradise'. In a fundamental sense, then, the 'hell' of human struggle can be said to have produced the 'heaven' of peace and harmony as its shadow or ideal other self, but to have disguised this by a mythological reversal whereby 'heaven' creates 'hell' as a punishment for rebellion or for refusal to be content. This leaves us with the paradox that we can admire Satan at this stage in the poem and be to some extent grateful for his fall, since otherwise we would not have the inspiring example of his heroism, courage, and struggle. To this extent, then, Satan's fall is 'fortunate', since it enabled human history to begin, and, further, the consequent fall of Adam and Eve enabled us to know good by the emergence of evil. Milton makes this case in arguing against censorship in 1644:

> It was from out the rinde of one apple tasted, that the knowledge of good and evill as two twins cleaving together leapt forth into the World. And perhaps this is that doom which *Adam* fell into of knowing good and evill, that is to say of knowing good by evill. As therefore the state of man now is; what wisdome can there be to choose, what continence to forbeare without the knowledge of evill? He that can apprehend and consider vice with all her baits and seeming pleasures, and yet abstain, and yet distinguish, and yet prefer that which is truly better, he is the true

warfaring Christian. I cannot praise a fugitive and cloister'd vertue, unexercis'd & unbreath'd, that never sallies out and sees her adversary ... that which purifies us is triall, and triall is by what is contrary.[4]

Thus our perception of Satan in *Paradise Lost* cannot be simple-minded: in him we see the complex relationship of evil and good, and it is only through his fall that we can recognize the distinction between them, difficult though this is.

Satan makes his first grand speech in addressing his colleague Beelzebub. At first he hardly recognizes him – 'If thou beest he' (I. 84) – but then he remembers him in terms of light, 'clothed with transcendent brightness' (I. 86), reminding us of how recent was their loss of heaven, after nine days falling (VI. 871) and nine days in the fiery gulf (I. 50). This speech breathes defiance: he defends the war ('till then who knew/The force of those dire arms' (I. 94)), argues that it was a popular cause ('Innumerable force of spirits armed/That durst dislike his reign' (I. 101–2)), and claims that they did not do too badly ('And shook his throne' (I. 105)). It is worth remembering that Milton too had supported a party in 1649 which had 'utmost power with adverse power opposed' (I. 103) and had shaken the throne of Charles I. Now also for Milton in the late 1650s the field was clearly lost in the sense that the Revolution had failed. One reaction might have been in accord with the proud, inspirational, public rhetoric of Satan at this point:

> *What though the field be lost?*
> *All is not lost; the unconquerable will,*
> *And study of revenge, immortal hate,*
> *And courage never to submit or yield:*
> *And what is else not to be overcome?*
>
> (I. 105–9)

(The primary meaning of that last line seems to be 'What does "not to be overcome" mean, otherwise?') Milton *did* remain implacably opposed to the English monarchy, but the crucial difference here between Satan's position and Milton's is that Satan has identified the wrong enemy, and is supporting the wrong cause – essentially himself and his sense of 'injured merit' (I. 98). Whatever the ultilmate power in the universe is, and however we name it, to oppose it implacably with injured self-regard as a motive is to put passion above reason. In this sense 'God' must be obeyed. Milton never regarded the English monarchy as representing the Almighty (which was how it regarded itself), and in fact we may see in Satan in the first two books of the poem some allusion to Charles I, in his regal bearing before his baronial court, as a rebel against God's will for his English people. Satan's speech here, punctuated by rhetorical questions in the manner of the demagogue, produces a strong sense of relentless resistance, but no sense of anything superior to the 'tyranny of Heaven' (I. 124), his last words. Milton has defined a 'tyrant' for us: 'A Tyrant whether by wrong or by right coming to the Crown, is he who regarding neither Law nor the common good, reigns for himself and his faction'.[5] This is Satan, whose private face is glimpsed briefly at this point, 'racked with deep despair' (I. 126).

Beelzebub, however, is not quite so sure that 'to undergo eternal punishment' (I. 155) is such a good idea. His speech again worries at the issue of the possible omnipotence of God. He gives formal praise to Satan for having 'endangered heaven's perpetual king' (I. 131), but concludes their defeat to be a proof of God's almightiness, and therefore can see no point in a life of servitude in hell. The question is raised as to whether God's supremacy is upheld 'by strength, or chance, or fate' (I. 133), a question which, as we have seen, is at the heart of the poem. 'Strength' is Beelzebub's implied answer. Satan's retort to Beelzebub sounds like the aside of a melodramatic stage villain: 'To do aught good never will be our task,/But ever to do ill our sole delight' (I. 159–60), but in fact it defines the endless struggle between good and evil which characterizes human history:

If then his providence
Out of our evil seek to bring forth good,
Our labour must be to pervert that end,
And out of good still to find means of evil.

(I. 162–5)

The 'Fortunate Fall' is thus a doctrine Satan seems to know all about.

Epic, like other literary or narrative forms, whether in verse, prose, film, or other media, is recognizable because it adheres to certain *conventions*, or stylistic features which distinguish it from other forms, or from everyday uses of language. Milton's opening outline of the action of *Paradise Lost* (I. 1–26) and the address to the muse (I. 1–49) are, for example, conventional openings similar to those which had been used by Homer in the *Iliad*, and Virgil in the *Aeneid*. One of the most notable stylistic features of epic is the figure of speech by which an extended comparison, or simile, is so elaborated that it dominates the original point of comparison through its vividness or ingenuity. The epic simile thus adds impact, as well as adding an incidentally decorative element to the texture of the poem. There are about two hundred examples in the 16,000 lines of the *Iliad*; in

Paradise Lost there are more epic similes concerned with aspects of Satan than with any other topic. There are none at all relating to God or the Son.

In Book I the epic similes relating to Satan and his angels emphasize mainly Satan's large size and the large number of the angels. Lines 192–210 produce a sense of Satan's immensity by comparing him first with the Titans of classical legend, and then with the biblical Leviathan, supposedly the largest creature made by God, this latter image being vividly elaborated by reference to the seamen's tale of the skiff anchoring in his 'scaly rind' (I. 206). Thus we are given, not a *description* of Satan, but an *impression*, alluding to pagan and biblical sources, as well as to sailors' gossip. When Satan moves to rouse his legions, his own size is emphasized by the similes of the moon-sized shield (the moon imagined as seen through the newly developed telescope of Galileo, the 'Tuscan artist' (I. 288)), and of his larger-than-tree-sized spear. The numerousness of his legions, their posture, and, possibly, their implicit association with death, are emphasized by the references to autumnal leaves on the brooks in Vallombrosa, near Florence. (It is of interest to find Milton processing memories of his Italian journey of 1638–9 here, as well as in the previous reference to Galileo, whom he met at Fiesole, near Florence, and also possibly in the imagery of the fiery gulf of hell, which may derive from a visit to the volcanic scenery near Naples.) Then, in a series of three similes, ascending from plant, to insect, to human imagery, his legions are likened to 'scattered sedge' on the Red Sea (I. 304–11), the cloud of locusts which plagued Egypt (I. 338–43), and finally to the barbarians who poured south across Europe in the centuries after Christ (I. 351–5). The overall effect of this accumulation of similes is to reinforce the number and moral disreputableness of Satan's supporters, together, possibly, with an implication of necromancy in their progression under the 'uplifted spear/Of their great sultan' (I. 347–8). What in another context might be a 'mixed metaphor' has, in an epic context such as this, a cumulative effect – though we might notice that there are certain critical problems connected with the extent of the intended relevance of Milton's similes. For example, it is the 'rod/Of Amram's son' (I. 338–9), i.e. Moses, which calls up the locusts: is Satan being compared here with Moses? Surely not: it must rather be the *contrast* with Moses that we are asked to notice. Further, how can *anything* pour 'from frozen loins' (I. 352)? The image is presumably a parody of the fertility usually associated with the sun. Whatever our judgment, we notice now that Satan's chains, which formerly tied him to the burning lake (I. 210), have disappeared, and we might in retrospect see them as a metaphor for the drugged state out of which he rouses first himself and then his followers. (In Book II, Moloch refers to 'the sleepy drench/Of that forgetful lake' (II. 73–4).)

At this point a major problem arises for modern readers of the poem. It is the question why, or whether, God allowed Satan to rise from the burning lake. We are told in Book I that he would never have left the flaming place

. . . but that the will
And high permission of all-ruling heaven
Left him at large to his own dark designs,
That with reiterated crimes he might
Heap on himself damnation, while he sought
Evil to others, and enraged might see
How all his malice served but to bring forth
Infinite goodness, grace and mercy shown
On man by him seduced, but on himself
Treble confusion, wrath and vengeance poured.

(I. 211–20)

But is not God here, as William Empson argues in his book *Milton's God*, presented as deliberately and maliciously leading Satan into greater evil? And might this not further imply that the three-day War in Heaven itself was a calculated deceit on the part of omnipotent God to make Satan believe victory was possible? Further, there seems to be a contradiction here with the words of God himself in Book III, where he says:

Only begotten Son, seest thou what rage
Transports our adversary, whom no bounds
Prescribed, no bars of hell, nor all the chains
Heaped on him there, nor yet the main abyss
Wide interrupt can hold; so bent he seems
On desperate revenge, that shall redound
Upon his own rebellious head.

(III. 80–86)

Did Satan have God's 'permission' to escape, or were the chains not strong enough to restrain him? The explanations for this discrepancy may be condensed into three. One is that Milton made a mistake, and forgot his story. However, the power of the verse at this point seems to contradict the view that Milton was nodding off, and implies that the passage in Book III meant something important to him. Christopher Ricks has demonstrated, for example, how the word 'transports' (III. 81) compresses the idea of both motion and emotion, and has pointed out how 'can hold' (III. 84) seems to fly free of the heaped chains of the earlier part of the clause.[6] A second explanation is that this is one of 'God's grisly jokes' (the phrase is William Empson's), and that God is really allowing Satan the space to make himself ridiculous while sardonically pretending that no bounds, bars, or chains can hold him. A third explanation is that the speech of God is part of 'the hypocrisy which the jovial old ruffian feels to be required of him in public', and which allows him to impress the loyalist angels who are listening with the justness of his revenge on Satan.[7] None of these explanations is, however, entirely satisfactory, since the very problem of the discrepancy arises inevitably from Milton's decision to make God speak. This means that God, the supreme omniscient and omnipotent presence, becomes a 'person' with knowledge, intentions, motives, and emotions, and takes his place as part of a narrative with other 'persons'. In such a situation, the poem's attempt to 'justify the ways of God' (I. 26) becomes exposed as inherently flawed, if not impossible.

Milton's struggle to make omniscient omnipotence benign, in the context of a world of pain and sorrow, is not easy, even in theological terms, and concepts such as divine 'foreknowledge' (i.e. the idea that God might 'foreknow' something such as the Fall, and not prevent it, despite his omnipotence) and the 'Fortunate Fall', may be seen as theological attempts to rescue the idea of a benevolent omnipotence from the tendency of the evidence to the contrary. When made into a narrative, however, with speaking characters and a sequence of cause and effect, the problems and contradictions of asserting eternal providence and justifying the ways of God come very close to the surface, and are part of what make *Paradise Lost* of fascinating interest. We will return to this topic in considering Book III.

Though personalizing omnipotence creates insoluble problems, Satan the rebel is powerfully presented as a person: the supreme individualist. He rebels against powers whose extent he is not sure of, but he is implacably determined to be 'free'. His speech is awesomely magnificent on leaving the burning lake, but on closer inspection raises interesting problems:

Farewell happy fields
Where joy for ever dwells: hail horrors, hail
Infernal world, and thou profoundest hell
Receive thy new possessor: one who brings
A mind not to be changed by place or time.
The mind is its own place, and in itself
Can make a heaven of hell, a hell of heaven.
What matter where, if I be still the same,

And what I should be, all but less than he
Whom thunder hath made greater? Here at least
We shall be free; the almighty hath not built
Here for his envy, will not drive us hence:
Here we may reign secure, and in my choice
To reign is worth ambition though in hell:
Better to reign in hell, than serve in heaven.

(I. 249–63)

('All but less than' seems to be a combination of 'all but equal to' and 'only less than', and the use of 'almighty' is presumably ironic.) Satan's stirring rhetoric here is of independent identity, and freedom, and, for himself, monarchy. There is, of course, a logical contradiction between speaking on behalf of independence and freedom, and wishing to reign. Satan himself points this out, as reported by Raphael, in criticizing God's coronation of his Son (which was the reason for Satan's rebellion in the first place):

Who can in reason then or right assume
Monarchy over such as live by right
His equals, if in power and splendour less,
In freedom equal?

(V. 794–7)

Satan's slippage in the speech quoted above from 'I' to 'we' seems to be an assumption of the royal plural, as he simultaneously asserts his independence in phrases such as 'the mind is its own place', 'if I be still the same', and 'here at least/We shall be free'. The defiance in the speech is as strong as Milton's of the English monarchy, but, as Abdiel (who was the one faithful seraph among Satan's faithless legions and, seemingly, a mouthpiece for Milton himself) explains direct to Satan:

This is servitude,
To serve the unwise, or him who hath rebelled
Against his worthier, as thine now serve thee,
Thy self not free, but to thy self enthralled.

(VI. 178–81)

Milton's concept of freedom will be considered more fully in discussing Books V and VI, but it involves much more than the mere absence of restraint, which Satan imagines, and which Milton would call 'licence'. Satan's words reflect his assumption that he is naturally and in principle independent of others, and this is sometimes called 'bourgeois individualism' since 'standing on your own two feet' and 'looking after yourself' have become standard philosophical assumptions about the individual in bourgeois society. John Locke in 1690 wrote a treatise attacking the absolute monarchy of the Stuarts and in favour of a constitutional monarchy. He argued that man in a 'state of Nature' is 'absolute lord of his own person and possessions, equal to the greatest and subject to nobody', but that, for the sake of the security of Law, men enter into society, except, that is, for the absolute monarch, who remains in a state of nature, subject to no law but himself.[8] This is Satan's concept of freedom: in reality 'enthralled to himself'. In a more general sense we may see in Satan's position that perennial utopian illusion that an 'individual' can by an act of will become free of all the social and cultural, including linguistic, forces that make us what we are. This is an illusion because, put simply, human life is always *contingent*, character is always *produced* by forces that we often choose not to recognize, or are ignorant of. Like Satan.

In the second book of the *Iliad* Homer writes:

> Tell me now, you Muses that live on Olympus, since you are goddesses and witness all that happens, whereas we men know nothing that we are not told – tell me who were the captains and chieftains of the Danaans. As for the rank and file that came to Ilium, I could not name or even count them, not if I had ten tongues, ten mouths, a voice that could not tire, a heart of bronze, unless you Muses of Olympus, Daughters of aegis-bearing Zeus, would serve me as remembrancers.[9]

Homer then over several hundred lines lists the Danaan (i.e. Greek), and then the Trojan, leaders. For the knowledgeable, the list of names is both resonant with associations and imposing in its length. Milton's catalogue of the Fallen Angels is similarly introduced, and fulfils an analogous function:

> *Say, Muse, their names then known, who first, who last,*
> *Roused from the slumber, on that fiery couch,*
> *At their great emperor's call, as next in worth*
> *Came singly where he stood on the bare strand,*
> *While the promiscuous crowd stood yet aloof'*
>
> (I. 376–80)

Milton's catalogue is not of heroes, of course, but of degenerates: the epithets 'horrid ... grim ... obscene ... lustful ... odious ... monstrous ... brutish ... lewd' set the dominant tone. We do not need to recognize every name or reference to sense the significance of what is going on. The muse is foreseeing the future names and reputations of Satan's army in the idolatry of paganism. There are twelve names in the list: Moloch, Chemos, Baalim, Ashtaroth, Astoreth, Thammuz, Dagon, Rimmon, Osiris, Isis, Horus, and Belial; and the whole seems to be intended as an infernal parody of Christ's calling of his twelve disciples. The first and last of the list figure again in Book II. Moloch, the first, is a savage and primitive deity 'besmeared with blood/Of human sacrifice' (I. 392–3), whereas Belial, the last, is a 'lewd' spirit whose name is a personification of sophisticated decadence, a corruption far removed from savagery: 'In courts and palaces he also reigns/And in luxurious cities' (I. 497–8). We therefore might be able to guess in advance the nature of the arguments which they will put forward in the council in Book II.

These future identities of the fallen angels are not yet manifest, however, as they rouse themselves from their slumber. Milton gives a magnificent picture of the military strength of the army as Satan raises the morale of his troops and as they organize themselves. He 'gently raised/Their fainting courage' (I. 529–30), and that verb 'raised' sets the theme for the upward movement of the recovery of the angels: 'upreared ... tall ... high advanced ... upsent ... rise ... rose ... raised' (I. 532–51). Like the army of the loyalist angels, whom we hear about later in Book VI, Satan's angels move in silence to the sound of soft music, and in a 'phalanx', a battle formation common in Milton's time. Only a hundred lines previously, however, we have been told that

> *... spirits when they please*
> *Can either sex assume, or both; so soft*
> *And uncompounded is their essence pure,*
> *Not tied or manacled with joint or limb,*
> *Nor founded on the brittle strength of bones,*
> *Like cumbrous flesh; but in what shape they choose*
> *Dilated or condensed, bright or obscure,*
> *Can execute their airy purposes,*
> *And works of love or enmity fulfil.*
>
> (I. 423–31)

Therefore their military formations and weapons must be symbolic, an anticipation of human warfare. Their 'embodied force' (I. 574), we are told, exceeded that of all armies seen since the creation of man, including those 'in fable or romance' (I. 580).

Satan as military commander, as public presence, is again described in images of impressive scale, the simile of the tower (I. 591) being followed by that of the hazy sun and then the eclipse, when the sun 'disastrous twilight sheds/On half the nations, and with fear of change/Perplexes monarchs' (I. 597–9). The eclipse later becomes a symptom of the effect of the Fall on nature, thus providing an extra significance to the image at this point; these lines were also thought by Charles II's supporters to be politically subversive. Yet Satan's public impressiveness is allied to a privately remorseful sensitivity to the position of his faithful legions, who stand around him,

> *Their glory withered. As when heaven's fire*
> *Hath scathed the forest oaks, or mountain pines,*
> *With singed top their stately growth though bare*
> *Stands on the blasted heath.*
>
> (I. 612–15)

This image is a fine combination of stateliness and barrenness, with the trees, like the legions, standing on burnt ground. Satan tries three times to speak, but is choked by his tears. As a result, his morale-boosting speech is much quieter in tone than his earlier rousing imperatives ('Awake, arise, or be for ever fallen' (I. 330)). Satan now explains their defeat as the result of a deception by God, who 'his strength concealed,/Which tempted our attempt, and wrought our fall' (I. 641–2). (In Raphael's account later in the poem God certainly admits allowing the war to drag on to a third day in order to give his Son the glory of ending it (VI. 700–703).)

Satan now suggests a new strategy, a form of guerrilla warfare:

> *... our better part remains*
> *To work in close design, by fraud or guile*
> *What force effected not: that he no less*
> *At length from us may find, who overcomes*
> *By force, hath overcome but half his foe.*
> *Space may produce new worlds ...*
>
> (I. 645–50)

This, the first hint that the earth may have been created (during the fallen angels' stupor in the fiery gulf), involves mankind in Satan's war. 'For who can think submission?' he exclaims, 'War then, war/Open or understood must be resolved' (I. 661–2). Thus is confirmed the adversarial course of history.

3 Pandaemonium: I. 670–798

When Ovid presents the classical myth of the Four Ages of mankind's history (Gold, Silver, Bronze, and Iron), he presents the last, Iron, Age in part as follows:

Last of all arose the age of hard iron: immediately, in this period which took its name from a baser ore, all manner of crime broke out; modesty, truth, and loyalty fled. Treachery and trickery took their place, deceit and violence and criminal greed ... Nor was it only corn and their due nourishment that men demanded of the rich earth: they explored its very bowels, and dug out the wealth which it had hidden away, close to the Stygian shades; and this wealth was a further incitement to wickedness.[10]

Here is the association of wealth with hell ('the Stygian shades'), and of wealth with aggression. These associations Milton presents as Mammon's legacy to mankind:

... by him first
Men also, and by his suggestion taught,
Ransacked the centre, and with impious hands
Rifled the bowels of their mother earth
For treasures better hid. Soon had his crew
Opened into the hill a spacious wound
And digged out ribs of gold.

(I. 684–90)

'Ransacked ... rifled ... wound' – this assault on 'mother earth' is suggestively enriched by the allusive association of 'ribs' with Eve, the mother of mankind, formed from the rib of Adam.

Now, following much intense activity, a fabulous edifice arises, of extraordinary magnificence, as if by magic, 'like an exhalation, with the sound/Of dulcet symphonies and voices sweet' (I. 711–12). When the doors open, we discover here, in hell, an imitation heaven:

...from the arched roof
Pendent by subtle magic many a row
Of starry lamps and blazing cressets fed
With naphtha and asphaltus yielded light
As from a sky.

(I. 726–30)

Pandaemonium arises like the elaborate sets in a seventeenth-century masque. It is insubstantial, like an 'exhalation', and built 'like a temple'. The model for the description may be St Peter's Basilica, which Milton doubtless saw when he visited Rome, though it was at that time unfinished. The pilasters, the embossed and gilded roof, the brazen doors, and the lights are all details that correspond, though Doric pillars were not added to the piazza of St Peter's until about the time Milton was writing. Even the simile of the bees (I. 768–75), to which the fallen angels are likened, emphasizing their business and comparative smallness compared with the immensity of the building, lends weight to the comparison, since the emblem of Pope Urban VIII, the founder of St Peter's, was the bee, and his followers were as a result often nicknamed 'bees'. The separate and adjacent Council Chamber, on this reading, corresponds to the Vatican (the library of which Milton had visited), and Milton's anti-Catholicism is reinforced by the words used of Satan's council, which sat 'in close recess and secret conclave' (I. 795) – phrases associated for Protestants with Jesuit plottings or the election of a pope by the College of Cardinals.

The angel-architect who designed Pandaemonium, who had formerly been an important architect in heaven, later became known in Italy ('Ausonian land'), we are told, as Mulciber. Homer's account of the fall of Hephaistos (Mulciber's Greek name) is the basis for Milton's striking version of the same event. Hephaistos addresses his mother:

> The Olympian is a hard god to pit oneself against. Why, once before when I was trying hard to save you, he seized me by the foot and hurled me from the threshold of Heaven. I flew all day, and as the sun sank I fell half-dead in Lemnos, where I was picked up and looked after by the Sintians.[11]

Notice now how Milton uses the devices of rhythm and selective epithets ('crystal', 'dewy'), together with a change in perspective (from above to below), to create the sense of a Mediterranean summer's day, and then abruptly to cut it off:

> *Men called him Mulciber; and how he fell*
> *From heaven, they fabled, thrown by angry Jove*
> *Sheer o'er the crystal battlements; from morn*
> *To noon he fell, from noon to dewy eve,*
> *A summer's day; and with the setting sun*
> *Dropped from the zenith like a falling star,*
> *On Lemnos the Aegaean isle: thus they relate,*
> *Erring; for he with this rebellious rout*
> *Fell long before; nor aught availed him now*
> *To have built in heaven high towers.*
>
> (I. 740–49)

That sudden brake on 'Erring' reminds us again that classical legends are only imperfect images of the truth, and brings us back to Milton's narrative. After the simile of the bees, the angels are suddenly reduced to a size 'less than the smallest dwarfs' (I. 779), and we may note here Milton's verbal play on 'smallest' and 'large':

> *Thus incorporeal spirits to smallest forms*
> *Reduced their shapes immense, and were at large,*

Though without number still amidst the hall
Of that infernal court.

(I. 789–92)

This is, as Christopher Ricks observes, a 'superbly contemptuous pun'.[12] Meanwhile the generals keep their own dimensions in council.

4 The Big Debate: II. 1–628

Is hell a parliamentary democracy, or a corrupt monarchy? Satan's first speech, from his exotic, glittering 'throne of royal state' (II. 1), claims his right to leadership on three grounds. These are: (i) the 'fixed laws of heaven', which he identifies with 'just right[ness]' (II. 18); (ii) the free choice of his followers, based on his merit 'in counsel or in fight' (II. 20); and, most important of all, (iii) the achievements of the rebels in recovering from the loss of heaven, which gives him 'a safe unenvied throne/Yielded with full consent' (II. 23–4). The class system in heaven is highly stratified, he claims, and therefore is likely to produce envy, whereas who would envy Satan's arduous role, who is exposed 'Foremost to stand against the thunderer's aim', and who is condemned to 'greatest share/Of endless pain'? (II. 28–30). Therefore, he argues, hell is more egalitarian, and has the advantage of a solidarity superior to that of class-divided heaven. He proposes, using the parliamentary terminology, that they 'debate' strategy (II. 42).

Just over ten years before Milton began writing *Paradise Lost*, the series of meetings of the recently established Council of the Army took place in St Mary's Church, Putney, in October and November 1647. Known as the 'Putney Debates', these meetings were called to discuss political demands – essentially the precise powers and limits of parliamentary government – and in attendance were army officers and elected representatives of the regiments, known as 'agitators', who were the main supporters of the radical group known as the Levellers. We may see in the debate in Pandaemonium an ironic parody of the debates in Putney. A pamphlet which was submitted to the Council of the Army for consideration at Putney, under the title *An Agreement of the People for a firme and present Peace, upon grounds of common-right and freedome*, basically the Leveller manifesto, states in the opening paragraph, 'We do now hold ourselves bound in mutual duty to each other, to take the best care we can for the future, to avoid both the danger of returning into a slavish condition, and the chargeable remedy of another war'. After specifying demands for representative parliaments and equality under the law, the pamphlet concludes:

> These things we declare to be our native Rights, and therefore are agreed and resolved to maintain them with our utmost possibilities, against all opposition whatsoever, being compelled thereunto, not only by the examples of our Ancestors ... but also by our own wofull experience, who having long expected & dearly earned the establishment of these certain rules of Government are yet made to depend for the settlement of our Peace and Freedome, upon him that intended our bondage, and brought a cruell Warre upon us.

This rhetoric of 'mutual duty', slavish bondage, utmost resistance, and imposed tyranny is all echoed by Satan, though, ironically, as part of an argument for continued war rather than peace. By 1658 it was becoming clear that providence had not favoured the revolutionary cause, so Satan's role here, in the trappings not merely of a monarch but of a stereotypical oriental tyrant, praising the egalitarianism of hell, embodies a significant contradiction.

This contradiction, between personal power and egalitarian talk, was Cromwell's as well as Satan's. Cromwell, in the Putney Debates, had expressed the view that giving voting rights to all men ('manhood suffrage'), including those who owned no land or property, 'did tend very much to Anarchy'.[13] He therefore was against the Levellers, who were in favour of manhood suffrage without a property qualification. Cromwell, in fact, came more and more to resemble a benevolent despot, governing increasingly by decree rather than by consultation, and, although he rejected the title of king which was urged on him in 1657, his personal authority was inevitably strengthened. His death the following year revealed that the regime had come to depend entirely on him personally, as the central authority collapsed after the deposition of his son within six months. In 1660 Milton wrote:

> Certainly then that people must needs be madd or strangely infatuated, that build the chief hope of thir common happiness or safetie on a single person: who if he happen to be good, can do no more then another man, if to be bad, hath in his hands to do more evil without check, then millions of other men. The happiness of a nation must needs be firmest and certainest in a full and free Councel of thir own electing, where no single person, but reason only swaies.[14]

Milton continued at this time, with the imminent restoration of the English monarchy, to advocate 'a frugal and selfgoverning democratie or Commonwealth, safer and more thriving in the joint providence and counsel of many industrious equals, then under the single domination of one imperious Lord'. It soon becomes clear that, despite appearances, Satan has manipulated the outcome of the debate in hell.

The first three speakers are Moloch, Belial, and Mammon, whom we might characterize, following William Empson, as, respectively, the General, the Lawyer, and the Industrialist.[15] Moloch, whom we remember as the 'horrid king besmeared with blood/Of human sacrifice' (I. 392–3), is a militarist, concerned only with proving his strength against God's in an all-or-nothing battle. He aggressively wastes no time on the formalities of parliamentary address: 'My sentence is for open war', he begins (II. 51). He despises strategists who 'sit contriving', thus obliging armies to 'sit lingering', and advocates that those 'millions that stand in arms' should 'ascend', which, he argues, is easy, since it is natural for angels to ascend (II. 54–81). Moloch's inflamed argument has a confident logic; their present situation, as slaves of 'his' anger, in unending pain, is the worst possible, so what is there to lose? Inciting 'him' to anger, therefore, will either end their misery by causing their destruction, or, if that proves impossible because their substance is immortal (a view expressed by Satan in I. 116–17), then ceaseless attacks on 'his' throne will provide the satisfaction at least of revenge, if not of victory.

The next speaker is the smooth-tongued Belial who, by contrast with Moloch, deploys all the sophisticated rhetorical skills of the barrister in his argument for endurance over force. He picks up Moloch's last word – 'revenge' (II. 105) – and argues that, though he himself is 'not behind in hate', the impossibility of reaching 'his' virtually impregnable throne would turn supposed revenge into 'flat despair'. Then in a relentless series of rhetorical questions he demolishes Moloch's argument. What advantage could it be to perish rather than to exist? Anyway, isn't it naive to imagine that 'he' would destroy them if that gave them what they wanted? 'He' is smarter than that. But what is so bad about the present situation, 'thus sitting, thus consulting, thus in arms'? Things could be very much worse. Then, with a brilliant stroke, Belial argues that God anyway knows what they are planning: 'He from heaven's highth/All these our motions vain, sees and derides'. Therefore *no* strategy will work, and so the wisest counsel is to endure, in the hope either that God will eventually be satisfied and 'remit/His anger', or that their pain will seem less as they get used to it. In any case, one never knows what might turn up if they do nothing reckless, or, in fact, nothing at all. Belial's is a shrewd argument, based on the premise that it is safest to assume that God is both omnipotent and omniscient.

Mammon is the third speaker, and, as we know already, he had the enterprise to organize the building of Pandaemonium itself. He follows

Belial in advocating peace rather than war, since their winning a war would depend on the unlikely event of 'everlasting fate', or providence, yielding to 'fickle chance'. But, much more positive than Belial, Mammon the businessman argues for capital investment in hell, rather than hoping for some 'wearisome eternity' worshipping a hated God. The devils now have, he argues, the chance to be free, 'preferring/Hard liberty before the easy yoke/Of servile pomp', and they have the intellectual, artistic, and physical resources 'to raise/Magnificence; and what can heaven show more?'. Mammon's anti-war policy based on founding a rival empire to that of heaven gets the applause of the council. It is a policy not merely of endurance, as was Belial's, but of 'labour and endurance' (II. 262).

Beelzebub next rises to his feet, manifestly worried by the apparent popularity of the peace movement. His argument, as we later learn 'devised/By Satan' (II. 380), is against open war with God, but also against establishing a 'growing empire' in hell, since this will merely extend 'his' empire, and result in their endless slavery and punishment. The clever course is to find God's weak spot: and Beelzebub repeats the rumour already mentioned by Satan (in I. 651–6) that God's anciently announced new world was already, or would soon be, created. We remember that Satan had suggested that God would favour the new race 'equal to the sons of heaven' (I. 654); Beelzebub, however, inflates this to 'favoured more/Of him who rules above' (II. 350–51). That is how rumours grow. This new creation, 'less in power and excellence' than the angels, may therefore be vulnerable to either destruction or seduction, he suggests, and to wreck God's work would be to exact exquisite revenge. 'To sit in darkness here/Hatching vain empires' is as nothing to this prospect. They vote unanimously in favour.

For the reader at this point an uncomfortable problem arises in connection with the fact that God's intention to create humans was made in 'ancient' times (II. 346). Later in the poem Raphael reports God as claiming that the creation of man was intended as a replacement for the fallen angels, thereby preventing Satan from being proud of the harm he would have done in depopulating heaven (VII. 150–56). Does this therefore mean that God somehow *planned* the rebellion of Satan and his followers from ancient times? The way Milton escapes from this problem with his narrative is to make a clear separation of the concept of God's 'foreknowledge' from his omnipotent power to predestine. This is elaborated in Book III.

Beelzebub now addresses the question of who shall be sent in search of this new world. This may well have been agreed in advance with Satan, since, far from emphasizing the vulnerability of earth, as he had previously

(II. 360–62), he now stresses the hazards of evading its sentries (II. 410–413), which sufficiently stuns the council to allow Satan the space, 'with monarchal pride', to suggest himself for the journey. Though this possible collusion between Satan and Beelzebub might be considered a devilish deception of the council, it could also be seen as part of a normal process of public persuasion: Satan does, after all, volunteer himself, and the proposal allows him to lead from the front, even when it involves taking enormous risks such as disappearance in the black hole of non-existence. He is still at this point heroic:

> *But I should ill become this throne, O peers,*
> *And this imperial sovereignty, adorned*
> *With splendour, armed with power, if aught proposed*
> *And judged of public moment, in the shape*
> *Of difficulty or danger could deter*
> *Me from attempting.*
> (II. 445–50)

This self-sacrifice of Satan's is accompanied by the sound of remote thunder (II. 477), as is the Fall of Adam and Eve (IX. 1002), and, in a parodic parallel to the later self-sacrifice of the Messiah, the devils 'extol him equal to the highest in heaven' (II. 479). There is no doubting that Satan is at this point a 'matchless chief' in putting the interests of the group above his own safety, and the poem's narrative voice explicitly comments that the devils have not lost all their virtue (II. 482–3). But there are warnings for men in what has happened. One is that men's worthy ('specious' (II. 484) – the word has changed its meaning) deeds on earth may be a cover for secret ('close' (II. 485)) ambition. Another, emphasizing the devils' virtue, is embodied in the frustrated expostulation in which we might see Milton's regret at the failure of the English Revolution in which he had played so committed a part:

> *O shame to men! Devil with devil damned*
> *Firm concord holds, men only disagree*
> *Of creatures rational, though under hope*
> *Of heavenly grace: and God proclaiming peace,*
> *Yet live in hatred, enmity, and strife*
> *Among themselves, and levy cruel wars,*
> *Wasting the earth, each other to destroy:*
> *As if (which might induce us to accord)*
> *Man had not hellish foes enow besides,*
> *That day and night for his destruction wait.*
> (II. 496–505)

Possibly, even, in the description of Satan's exit from the council chamber 'with pomp supreme' we may discern Milton's barely repressed disgust at the English people's fascination for the trappings of monarchy.

Throughout the big debate the speakers do not once refer to God as 'God'. They use terms such as 'the fierce foe' (II. 78), or 'king of heaven' (II. 229), or merely the third person pronoun or adjective 'he' or 'his'. In this way their discourse reassuringly implies equality by demoting God to the status of an unnamed rival ruler or usurper.

The devils now find entertainment to fill their time, the 'irksome hours', until Satan's return. We are now in a fallen world of time, which hangs heavy in hell. The sporting group organize races and military contests; the boisterous group produce signs of social disorder in wild uproar and the tearing up of hills; the aesthetic group sing songs harmoniously lamenting their fate; the philosophical group discourse about questions of providence and foreknowledge, free will and fate; while others explore hell. The philosophical group 'found no end, in wandering mazes lost' (II. 561), and this image anticipates Adam's reasoning after the Fall, when he comes to blame himself:

> *. . . all my evasions vain,*
> *And reasonings, though through mazes, lead me still*
> *But to my own conviction.* (X. 829–31)

But the same imagery of forlorn (or lost) restlessness describes the nightmare discoveries of the explorers of hell:

> *Thus roving on*
> *In confused march forlorn, the adventurous bands*
> *With shuddering horror pale, and eyes aghast*
> *Viewed first their lamentable lot, and found*
> *No rest: through many a dark and dreary vale*
> *They passed, and many a region dolorous,*
> *O'er many a frozen, many a fiery alp,*
> *Rocks, caves, lakes, fens, bogs, dens, and shades of death,*
> *A universe of death, which God by curse*
> *Created evil, for evil only good,*
> *Where all life dies, death lives, and nature breeds,*
> *Perverse, all monstrous, all prodigious things,*
> *Abominable, inutterable, and worse*
> *Than fables yet have feigned, or fear conceived.* (II. 614–27)

5 Satan's Journey to the Gates of Hell: II. 629–889

Satan's flight through hell brings him to the gates, which he finds guarded by two figures, a female called Sin and a male called Death. They turn out to be his forgotten children. The reader must here decide whether this extraordinary story is an allegorical 'interruption' in the epic poem, or, rather, an integral part of the epic texture. This need present no difficulty if we recognize the whole poem to be 'allusive': each supernatural being is both an independent 'character' and a site of relationships and qualities which allude to the present human world. Thus Sin and Death might be taken to allude to abstract concepts in the same way that Moloch, Belial, or Mammon allude to particular sets of values. At the same time, as characters they tell us about Satan's private relationships, while providing a parody of the heavenly Father–Son–Holy Spirit relationship. One question we might bear in mind when considering them as characters is why an all-knowing God should put the disreputable Sin in charge of hell's gates – almost as if he intended her to let her father through when the crucial time came.

There are three relevant references which provide the background for this episode. One is in the Bible, where James argues that it is not God who tempts mankind into sin:

> But every man is tempted, when he is drawn away of his own lust, and enticed. Then when lust hath conceived, it bringeth forth sin: and sin, when it is finished, bringeth forth death.
>
> (James I. 14, 15)

Another reference is the allegorical presentation in Spenser's poem *The Faerie Queene* of the monster called Errour:

> *Halfe like a serpent horribly displaide,*
> *But th'other halfe did woman's shape retaine,*
> *Most lothsom, filthie, foule, and full of vile disdaine.*
>
> (I. i. 14)

She also has a tail 'pointed with mortall sting', and swallows her young. A third reference is to the classical legend of the birth of the goddess Athena: she sprang fully armed from the head of Zeus, and thus had no mother. This story was sometimes taken by Christian theologians as an imperfect allegory of the generation of God's Son.

Satan courageously addresses the monstrous female Sin and the shapeless Death (shapeless perhaps because death is unrecognizable before it comes). Satan's taunt that the 'hell-born' should not 'contend with spirits of heaven' is countered by the returned taunt by Death that Satan is 'hell-doomed' and should watch his language (II. 687, 697). An impressive epic simile of two black clouds meeting over the Caspian emphasizes their threatening confrontation, which is interrupted by Sin, who addresses Satan as *her* father, and refers to Death as *his* son and then as *her* son (II. 727–8). Satan has obviously forgotten her, so she reminds him of the circumstances of her birth. It was at the assembly of seraphim called to plot against God, where she sprang out of his head, causing him at the time 'miserable pain' (II. 752). However, with her 'attractive graces', she soon became a secret lover of her father's, and eventually, after the War in Heaven and her appointment to her present post, she gave birth to their bastard, Death. He then raped his mother, which resulted in the birth, as she describes them, of

> *These yelling monsters that with ceaseless cry*
> *Surround me, as thou sawest, hourly conceived*
> *And hourly born, with sorrow infinite*
> *To me, for when they list into the womb*
> *That bred them they return, and howl and gnaw*
> *My bowels, their repast; then bursting forth*
> *Afresh with conscious terrors vex me round,*
> *That rest or intermission none I find.*
>
> (II. 795–802)

Thus is vividly dramatized the infiniteness of guilt or fear which attends sin.

Sin has none of the doubts about the immortality of the rebel angels such as had been expressed by the rebel leaders. 'For that mortal dint,/Save he who reigns above, none can resist', she advises her father, and she is firmly convinced of the immutability of 'fate', which is an outsider's name for providence (II. 813–14, 809). Satan, however, is not convinced that his cause is hopeless, and he persuades her to rebel against the commands of God 'who hates me' and let Satan out through the gates, with the promise that he will return and take them to earth,

> *. . . where thou and Death*
> *Shall dwell at ease, and up and down unseen*
> *Wing silently the buxom air, embalmed*
> *With odours; there ye shall be fed and filled*
> *Immeasurably, all things shall be your prey.*
>
> (II. 840–44, 857)

Has Satan here merely deceived Sin in order to gain his exit? Or does

Satan at this point feel malice towards mankind to the extent of wishing them to be the victims of Sin and Death, rather than merely to 'seduce them to our party' (II. 368)? Satan's plans for mankind did not previously include Sin and Death, because he had forgotten Sin and not met Death before, so this would suggest that, as a clever strategist, he is improvising for immediate advantage, rather than working to a tightly planned schedule. Just as, in the human story of Adam and Eve, the fruit of the forbidden tree 'brought death into the world, and all our woe', so here in the 'non-human' story of Satan, Sin's 'fatal key' becomes the 'sad instrument of all our woe', which eventually will allow Death into the world (I. 3; II. 872). At this fateful moment there is thunder as the gates open, just as there will later be at the moment of Adam's eating of the forbidden fruit (II. 882; IX. 1002). God is, we remember, known as the Thunderer (I. 93; II. 28).

6 Satan's Journey to the Edge of the Universe: II. 890–1055

Today's popular idea of the universe is of an infinite emptiness and silence: space. The philosophical implications we might draw from this view are various. We might assume the atheist's position that earth and human life are the vulnerable products of chance in an indifferent rather than benevolent environment; or, alternatively, we might take the religious view that earth and human life are significant examples of the spiritual possibilities which point to a divinely ordered cosmos. The interesting point is that, despite scientific advances in the discovery and understanding of the universe, we still need to produce meanings for ourselves from our images of the larger environment in which we exist, and these meanings do not depend on any truth 'out there'. The meanings are produced to satisfy a need for significance, and they are always part of an argument, part of a necessarily ceaseless struggle for truth. So it was also in the seventeenth century with Milton. Satan views from the gates of hell

> *... a dark*
> *Illimitable ocean without bound,*
> *Without dimension, where length, breadth, and highth*
> *And time and place are lost.*
>
> (II. 891–4)

But, rather than being a world of silence and emptiness, it is a place

> *... where eldest Night*
> *And Chaos, ancestors of Nature, hold*

Eternal anarchy, amidst the noise
Of endless wars, and by confusion stand.

(II. 894–7)

The philosophical implication of this view of the universe is that, without order and the exercise of God's goodness such as we see in the created universe, Chaos and Chance preside over horrifying confusion. Anarchy is a permanent threat, into which a world without providence is likely to degenerate.

Here we have a possible problem for Milton's theodicy (which means 'justification of God'). If disharmonious matter existed before God, so that creation was a question of producing order out of disorder, Nature out of its 'ancestors' Night and Chaos, then the doctrine of God's omnipotence seems to be powerfully undermined, since creation seems to be limited to 'making the best of a bad job'. Milton provides a resolution of this problem later, in Book VII. There Raphael quotes God as saying that he *fills* space, and that randomness and chaos are not outside him, but are merely those parts to which he does not choose to extend his form-giving goodness (VII. 168–73). Thus Chaos is potential, or unrealized, creation. It is appropriate that Satan, on his destructive mission, should journey through this 'abyss' of confusion and disorder. After the Fall, Adam likens himself to Satan, and exclaims:

O conscience! into what abyss of fears
And horrors hast thou driven me; out of which
I find no way, from deep to deeper plunged!

(X. 842–4)

Conscience was the 'umpire' God gave fallen mankind (III. 195); when Satan arrives on earth his 'conscience wakes despair' (IV. 23). The difference is that Satan rejects the voice of conscience, and thus discovers the 'hell within' (IV. 20, 75); Adam, however, is eventually promised a 'paradise within' (XII. 587).

We may notice how skilfully Milton presents Satan's hesitancy in entering Chaos:

Into this wild abyss,
The womb of nature and perhaps her grave,
Of neither sea, nor shore, nor air, nor fire,
But all these in their pregnant causes mixed
Confusedly, and which thus must ever fight,
Unless the almighty maker them ordain
His dark materials to create new worlds,

Into this wild abyss the wary fiend
Stood on the brink of hell and looked a while,
Pondering his voyage.

(II. 910–19)

The sense of movement implied in the first 'into this wild abyss' is held up for seven lines: but even then the repetition of the phrase is followed by the verb 'stood', which again holds up any movement, as does the next verb 'looked'. There follows an amazing journey through all the elements, of which one interesting feature is that the whole future history of mankind seems to have depended on one 'chance' thundercloud which prevents Satan from falling out of control (II.934–5). Meeting Chaos on his throne, Satan then asks for a guide to earth, promising, if he gets there, that he will reduce it to his sway: 'Yours be the advantage all, mine the revenge' (II. 987). Since Satan with the devils has already approved the plan to possess earth 'as our own' (II. 366), this seems to be a deception similar to that which he made on Sin in order to get out of hell (II. 840–41).

The big critical question is what deduction we draw from the fact of Satan's success in getting from hell to earth. William Empson argues that it is evidence of God's determination to make man fall:

> As a believer in the providence of God, Milton could not possibly have believed in the huge success-story of Satan fighting his way to Paradise. The chains of Hell, Sin, Death, Chaos and an army of good angels hold Satan back, but all this stage machinery is arranged by God to collapse as soon as he advances upon it.[16]

On the other hand, we may agree with Dennis Danielson, who argues that Chaos is 'a fine picture of any world without God', and is somehow analogous to free will:

> Milton keeps reminding us that the deep Satan has navigated continues to present both evil and good possibilities, which in Chaos as well as in creaturely freedom exist in poignant proximity ... Meanwhile, of course, for Adam and his race, the 'ever-threatening storms/Of Chaos' will bluster round (III. 425–6). But even in this fallen world, Chaos can be exploited for good by God, and by man in obedience to God. As Adam comes to recognize through Christ's example (XII. 561–79), suffering itself can be infused with meaning for the one who serves truth and is conscious of providential purpose.[17]

These opposing interpretations raise fundamental issues about how to read the poem, which demand to be confronted at the start of Book III.

Meanwhile, Satan, after great difficulty, finds, illuminated by the resplendent walls of heaven, 'hanging in a golden chain/This pendant world' (II, 1051–2). Thus the universe appears first in the poem, seen through the eyes of Satan.

III The Second Day: Heaven, Satan's Journey, and Paradise

1 Light: III. 1–55

The change of scene from the 'utter' darkness of hell and the 'middle' darkness of Chaos to heaven itself and the person of God is marked at the start of Book III by an address, or invocation, to Light (III. 16). Milton seems here variously to address Light as the Son of God ('offspring of heaven first-born' (III. 1)), as God himself ('God is light' (III. 3)), and as something of unknown origin ('whose fountain who shall tell?' (III. 8)). Whatever its nature, light is here both literal and symbolic. Literally, it is absent from Milton's life: '... but thou/Revisit'st not these eyes, that roll in vain/To find thy piercing ray, and find no dawn' (III. 22–4). Symbolically, this poignant absence of the literal phenomenon can be redeemed:

> *So much the rather thou celestial Light*
> *Shine inward, and the mind through all her powers*
> *Irradiate, there plant eyes, all mist from thence*
> *Purge and disperse, that I may see and tell*
> *Of things invisible to mortal sight.*
>
> (III. 51–5)

This claim, to be revealing the invisible, produces a critical problem for the reader. The 'inspired' narrative voice of the poem is often accused of making didactic interruptions to the story which prevent the narrative from 'speaking for itself'. Some examples from just the first two books are:

- the comment on Satan's first speech, which gave little if any evidence of despair, that he was 'vaunting aloud, but racked with deep despair' (I. 126);
- the reference to the impotence of his 'reiterated crimes' in I. 214–20;
- the comment on Satan's speech of exhortation to his army, that it 'bore/Semblance of worth, not substance' (I. 528–9);
- the comment following the vivid story of the fall of Mulciber: 'thus they relate,/Erring' (I. 746–7);
- the comment before Belial's speech, 'But all was false and hollow' (II. 112);

– the comment on the fallen angels' philosophical reasonings, 'Vain wisdom all, and false philosophy' (II. 565).

In addition to such comments there are the longer insertions into the poem of didactic reflections by the narrator, such as the one on the fallen angels' concord compared with man's disagreements in I. 496–505, and, later, the notable passage celebrating 'wedded love' in IV. 750–75. The critical problem is to know how we are to understand these observations.

One view is that adopted by Anne Ferry, who writes:

> We are meant to remember that the events of the poem have already occurred, to us and to the poet, and that it is because of what happens in the poem, because we and all men were corrupted by the Fall, that we stand in need of a guide to correct our reading of it. The narrative voice is our guide.[1]

This is a view which this book explicitly rejects, for several reasons. The first is that *Paradise Lost* is itself about the nature and exercise of authority, about who or what determines history, our lives, and moral values, and thus to submit unquestioningly to the authority of the 'narrative voice' is to short-circuit the whole narrative, by subordinating an understanding of its complexity to a desire for *religious* consolation. Of course, if the reader does hold such convictions about divine authority as are overtly described in the poem, then a refusal to recognize the authority of the 'narrative voice' will be regarded as satanic in its rebelliousness. But this is not really an argument about right or wrong 'beliefs' in the religious sense, but about ways of reading and comprehending a literary text. There are far more meanings produced by a written text than its formal 'message' can contain.

A second reason for rejecting the reading advocated by Anne Ferry above is that it assumes the literal truth of the characters and events in the poem, or at least of a historical Fall, which, she says, corrupted all men. In addition, presumably, the character of God is assumed, who was and is in charge and able to inspire an authoritative narrative voice. This is not a position easily defended in the face of modern scholarship, and in a predominantly non-believing culture.

A third reason for doubt about complete reliance on the authority of the didactic voice in the poem relates to the way language, particularly poetic language, works. Words are a feeble way of reflecting, let alone reproducing, reality, and often, after processing by a reader, produce implications or connotations quite at variance with the writer's intention. That is surely why Milton inserts a dominant narrative voice in the poem: in order to correct the tendency of the narration, lest, for example, we begin to think too highly of Satan. But the narrative voice itself, as part of the poem, needs precisely such correction, and needs to be read as part of the *problem* of the poem, not as its *solution* which tells us what to think.

A fourth reason for taking this line is that there is a discernible contradiction in Milton himself with regard to the ideology of the narrative voice. Consider these lines which follow the invocation to Light:

> *Thus with the year*
> *Seasons return, but not to me returns*
> *Day, or the sweet approach of even or morn,*
> *Or sight of vernal bloom, or summer's rose,*
> *Or flocks, or herds, or human face divine;*
> *But cloud in stead, and ever-during dark*
> *Surrounds me, from the cheerful ways of men*
> *Cut off . . .*
>
> (III. 40–47)

Milton is here nostalgic for the changing seasons, yet they were actually part of the *penalty* imposed as a result of the Fall (X. 678–9). Likewise agriculture was another result of the Fall, yet here Milton seems to miss the sight of 'flocks, or herds', and regrets being cut off from the 'cheerful ways of men', fallen men. Thus, while the narrative voice deplores the Fall, the human writer rejoices in its consequences. Reading a poem is altogether a more complicated matter than being obedient and thinking what we are told to think.

2 God: III. 56–415

The poem now turns to the presentation of God himself. In this task Milton faced problems to which he found no solution. He was not obliged to present God as a speaking character at all: the arguments about free will and foreknowledge could have been reported by the Son or other angels. The God which the angels praise is described as

> *. . . omnipotent,*
> *Immutable, immortal, infinite,*
> *Eternal king; thee author of all being,*
> *Fountain of light, thy self invisible*
> *Amidst the glorious brightness where thou sit'st*
> *Throned inaccessible . . .*
>
> (III. 372–7)

The God which Milton actually presents, however, cannot be 'immutable' since he experiences and displays emotions: Satan referred to the 'potent victor in his rage' (I. 95), Raphael later suggests that he was subject to uncontrollable rage (VIII. 235–6), and Sin reported how he 'laughs' (II. 731), for example; and it is hard to think of him as 'infinite' and 'invisible' when we are told that he 'bent down his eye' to view his works (III. 58). Even more difficult is the old theological problem of an 'omnipotent' being, who by definition could produce any world he chose, actually producing a world in which evil appears, and then punishing it with human death in the name of 'justice'. His 'goodness' must indeed seem a little suspect and in need of justification to men.

But the major problem with Milton's presentation of God is connected with God's use of language as a speaking and acting character in a narrative. All speech says more than appears on the surface: our language provides ineradicable traces of mood, register, dialect, intention, and attitude, and all these are attributes of weak, mutable, mortal, finite, and visible human beings. To give God language, and thereby emotions and intentionality, and to make him in that language justify theological paradoxes, is to betray the ideological project of social control involved in the invention of the idea of an implacable, immutable, immortal and infinite being. Language makes him human and thus fallible, since language, even the formal, non-metaphorical language used by God in this poem, *always* exists before the speaker, is *always* learned from other speakers, and thus always comes with its own history, never innocently, to the lips. If we work backwards from our own experience and invent the notion of a force that controls human history and destiny, an ultimate 'authority', such a force or authority cannot be personal, with all the human limitations of mutability and finiteness which that implies. If it is presented as personal then inevitably a ludicrous situation results: it is this which enables William Empson to find Milton's picture of God 'astonishingly like Uncle Joe Stalin; the same patience under an appearance of roughness, the same flashes of joviality, the same thorough unscrupulousness, the same real bad temper'.[2]

As we meet him now in Book III, God observes 'our two first parents' on earth – indicating that the creation of Adam and Eve has taken place – and also sees Satan, who has broken out of all the 'bounds/Prescribed', and is now on the edge of the universe (III. 65, 81–2). What might seem shocking at first to the reader is that, though God knows Satan will be successful in seducing mankind, he seems more concerned with defending his own blamelessness in the Fall:

> *... whose fault?*
> *Whose but his own? Ingrate, he had of me*

> *All he could have; I made him just and right,*
> *Sufficient to have stood, though free to fall.*
>
> (III. 96–9)

However, behind this impression, what we are really witnessing is Milton addressing the harsh question of blame for human failure, such as the failure of the English Revolution, and defending the idea of the Christian God, without whom the world would seem to disintegrate in moral chaos. Milton's 'rescue' of God results from the following reasoning. Obviously, if free will serves 'necessity' it is not free, therefore it must be possible for Adam and Eve to fall, and therefore God's omnipotence must not overrule their free will. But the alternative to a passively obedient Adam and Eve is not necessarily that God should be taken by surprise by the Fall. God's 'escape clause', which absolves him from the charge of responsibility for the Fall (i.e. that he predestined it), as well as from the charge of irresponsibility in allowing it (i.e. that his creative powers were at fault), is the concept of his 'foreknowledge', or omniscience. Thus God's omnipotence is intact, and he can know the Fall will happen, though it will not be his fault:

> *Foreknowledge had no influence on their fault,*
> *Which had no less proved certain unforeknown . . .*
> *They trespass, authors to themselves in all*
> *Both what they judge and what they choose; for so*
> *I formed them free, and free they must remain,*
> *Till they enthrall themselves: I else must change*
> *Their nature, and revoke the high decree*
> *Unchangeable, eternal, which ordained*
> *Their freedom, they themselves ordained their fall.*
>
> (III. 118–28)

He continues by explaining the one advantage that humans will have in his eyes when they fall, over the already fallen angels, which is that the angels were disobedient 'by their own suggestion', whereas man will fall 'deceived/By the other [i.e. the angels] first' (III. 129–31). This justifies God's 'mercy', of which he is proud. This line of reasoning causes severe problems for the mechanics of Milton's narrative as we have already noted above, since our omnipotent God must forbid Satan from tempting Eve at the same time as making sure that he can do so because he has 'foreseen' that he will.

The Son now responds to God's explanation of his position by arguing that if mankind were drawn to hell by Satan, or even exterminated by

God (a possibility already suggested by Beelzebub in II. 367–70), then God's goodness and greatness would suffer a serious blow. The Son speaks God's thoughts which his 'eternal purpose hath decreed' (III. 172). God now articulates the doctrine of his 'grace' which is the only hope for mankind. Some will be 'elect above the rest'; but, for the majority, God will be responsive to 'prayer, repentance, and obedience' (III. 184, 191). Further,

> *. . . I will place within them as a guide*
> *My umpire conscience, whom if they will hear,*
> *Light after light well used they shall attain,*
> *And to the end persisting, safe arrive.*
>
> (III. 194–7)

We may perhaps read in this Milton's aspiration for himself to be both 'elect' and 'to the end persisting', since the larger movement of the poem is towards making salvation not a public matter of setting up a commonwealth in England, but a private and solitary matter of prayer, repentance, and obedience.

God immediately turns harsh, however. Those who do not respond will be 'hardened' and blinded more, 'that they may stumble on, and deeper fall' (III. 201), and, for man's crime-to-be, which is now identified as treason,

> *He with his whole posterity must die,*
> *Die he or justice must; unless for him*
> *Some other able, and as willing, pay*
> *The rigid satisfaction, death for death.*
>
> (III. 209–12)

This 'rigid satisfaction' is a peculiar form of justice: death is not a *punishment*, but a *satisfaction* for the treason. In other words, God cannot let man off, even after 'prayer, repentance, and obedience', because of this justice which he has created. A further satisfaction is required: 'death for death'.

The silence of the angels at this point, when a volunteer is required for a dangerous task (to become mortal 'to redeem man's mortal crime'), reminds us of the similar moment in the devils' council when 'all sat mute' when asked who would undertake the expedition against man (II. 420; III. 215). It is one of several parallels between Pandaemonium and heaven. Here the Son steps in and offers to become human and die, though of course he knows that it will not be a real death, but that he will 'rise victorious', give 'death his death's wound', and thus show the 'powers of darkness bound' (III. 250, 252, 256). At the end of history he will enter heaven with the redeemed, and then, hopefully, God's 'wrath shall be no more' (III. 264). Thus is God's providence demonstrated before the Fall has even occurred, and all hinges on the Son's exemplary obedience, which shines above his love (III. 268–9). God gives him the go-ahead. The virgin birth, when the Son comes to earth, will make him a 'second root' for the redemption of mankind (Adam was the first), and, as reward, the Son will be exalted:

> *Here shalt thou sit incarnate, here shalt reign*
> *Both God and man, Son both of God and man,*
> *Anointed universal king, all power*
> *I give thee, reign for ever, and assume*
> *Thy merits; under thee as head supreme*
> *Thrones, princedoms, powers, dominions I reduce:*
> *All knees to thee shall bow . . .*
>
> (III. 315–21)

This fateful moment of the exaltation of the Messiah, which moves from future ('shalt') to a timeless present ('give', 'reduce'), is an anticipation of the chronologically earlier exaltation of the Son, recounted later in the poem in V. 600ff., which Milton adduces, in common with some other seventeenth-century writers, as the cause of the War in Heaven. God continues here to summarize his divine plan, phrased in references from the Bible. The end result will be, he says, a 'new heaven and new earth, wherein the just shall dwell', at which time the Son will lay down his royal sceptre, since 'God shall be all in all' (III. 335, 341). This is presumably because, with the arrival of universal perfection, no authority, whether of God or of the Son, is needed. Not so much an abdication of God as a diffusion of godliness.

The angels' chorus then spends 'happy hours' singing the praises of God and of the Son (who, incidentally, is here referred to as 'of all creation first' (III. 383) – an anti-trinitarian implication). The episode provides a contrast with the way the devils fill their 'irksome hours' after their infernal council (II. 527). The angels sing of the Son as the agency of God's creation, as well as the military leader who crushed the angelic rebellion, and of his offer to die for mankind in order to 'appease thy [God's] wrath, and end the strife/Of mercy and justice in thy face discerned' (III. 406–7). Again, these references to God's 'wrath', his 'face', and his internal 'strife' are not easy to reconcile with the image of the 'author of all . . .

inaccessible' at the start of the song (III. 374–7). The Son, however, is more consistently portrayed: his strategic function in the story is as a heroic counterpart to Satan, though, since he cannot lose, he carries less dramatic charge than Satan.

3 Satan's Arrival on the Sun: III. 416–742

At the end of the heavenly council, counterpart to the council in hell in the previous book, the scene shifts back to Satan's continuing voyage of discovery. In an impressive epic simile he is likened to a vulture who has come 'from a region scarce of prey/To gorge the flesh of lambs or yeanling kids', an image which compresses the rapacity of Satan and the innocence of humans, as well as anticipating their later division into sheep and goats which results from his intervention (III. 433–4). A phantasm, or ghostly illusion, is then described, which will at some future time exist, called the 'Paradise of Fools' (III. 496). In this limbo will be found 'all things vain [i.e. 'empty'], and all who in vain things/Built their fond hopes of glory or lasting fame' (III. 448–9). Milton seems still to be addressing the pressing question of human failure, as of the English Revolution: in this limbo,

> *All who have their reward on earth, the fruits*
> *Of painful superstition and blind zeal,*
> *Nought seeking but the praise of men, here find*
> *Fit retribution, empty as their deeds.*
>
> (III. 489–95)

The 'Paradise of Fools' also gives Milton the chance to indulge in more mockery of Roman Catholicism and its corruptions:

> *. . .then might ye see*
> *Cowls, hoods and habits with their wearers tossed*
> *And fluttered into rags, then relics, beads,*
> *Indulgences, dispenses, pardons, bulls,*
> *The sport of winds; all these upwhirled aloft*
> *Fly o'er the backside of the world far off*
> *Into a limbo large and broad . . .*
>
> (III. 489–95)

With 'a gleam/Of dawning light' we are returned to the present (III. 499–500). Satan sees the gate of heaven, embellished with diamond and gold, together with the ladder from heaven to earth that Jacob was one day to dream of (Genesis 28:12), with inviting steps, up and down which angels were moving. A wide passage goes down to the earth from beneath the ladder, and on the bottom step Satan 'looks down with wonder at the sudden view/Of all this world at once', just like an explorer who, after a perilous journey through the night, sees at last the 'goodly prospect of some foreign land' (III, 542–3, 548). His wonder is soon surpassed by his envy. It is night-time in Paradise, and Satan stands 'above the circling canopy/Of night's extended shade', that is, on the other side of the earth from the sun (III. 556–7). At once he flies, on his space-journey through the created universe, past innumerable stars that seem like other worlds, until he arrives at 'the golden sun', which was most like heaven in splendour, and which 'gently warms/The universe, and to each inward part/... shoots invisible virtue' (III. 572, 583–6). Now comes a joke:

> *There lands the fiend, a spot like which perhaps*
> *Astronomer in the sun's lucent orb*
> *Through his glazed optic tube yet never saw.*
>
> (III. 588–90)

This is a reference to the 'sunspots' which had been discovered by Galileo and others, and which were thought by some to be a wicked challenge to the common religious view of the perfection of the sun as an image of God. Thus it is appropriate and amusing that Satan should be represented as a previously unseen 'spot'.

Satan, undazzled in the sun's perpetual noon, now sees a 'glorious angel' with a golden crown, shining hair, and feathered wings, apparently deep in thought. In order to ask directions to Paradise, Satan decides to change his shape, and chooses that of a very attractive 'stripling cherub' (III. 636). Cherubs were supposed to excel in knowledge, so that is an appropriate disguise for someone asking for information; 'stripling' might refer to the common representation of cherubs as winged children, though angels, we later learn, are 'self-begot' and therefore presumably have no childhood (V. 860). A more fundamental implication of this episode is that disguise itself, as a change of nature, is intrinsically evil, an aspect of hypocrisy. This is the first of Satan's several changes of form.

The glorious angel is the first unfallen angel to appear by name in the poem, and is the archangel Uriel, whose name means 'Light of God'. He turns at the sound of the 'cherub', who explains that he has an 'unspeakable desire' to see man, God's 'chief delight and favour', and asks where he dwells in order that he may admire him and praise God,

> *Who justly hath driven out his rebel foes*
> *To deepest hell, and to repair that loss*

Created this new happy race of men
To serve him better: wise are all his ways.
(III. 662, 664, 677–80)

Uriel is deceived: hypocrisy is 'the only evil that walks/Invisible', even to the sharpest-sighted spirit in heaven (III. 683–4). Our thoughts might here for a moment turn to Eve: if an archangel falls for Satan's line in deception, it might seem rather unfair to expect Eve, 'our credulous mother', to do any better (IX. 644). Uriel praises the 'cherub's' desire 'to know/The works of God, thereby to glorify/ The great work-master', and thereby ironically (since this is not Satan's true purpose in wishing to know) clarifies the difference between this knowledge and that forbidden sort, which we hear about in the next book, symbolized by the eating from the 'fatal tree' (III. 694–6; IV. 514–15). No 'knowledge' is innocent of purpose. In our world today, military research is heavily funded compared with other more peaceful areas of potential knowledge, which are starved of resources. Knowledge is always connected with, is even the foundation of, power. When it becomes subversive of order and thus threatening, as in Paradise, it is forbidden: here on the sun, however, it seems that it can only 'glorify the great work-master'. Thus it is encouraged. Uriel gives Satan not only directions to Paradise, but also a brief account of the creation. He concludes with a reference to the moon, which prevents an 'invasion' of the earth by night, an ironically appropriate image, considering Satan's true mission. Satan courteously bows low, and flies to the top of Niphates, the mountain from which the Tigris, the river of Paradise, reputedly took its origin (XI. 71).

4 Satan's Arrival on Earth: IV. 1–130

With Eden now in view, Satan begins the action in Book IV with an emotional speech. It is Satan's first private speech, and, without the need to keep up a public image for the sake of the morale of his followers, his 'conscience wakes despair' (IV. 23). The characters in *Paradise Lost* do not soliloquize until they have fallen, and in this book we observe a big change in Satan. This is both physical, in that he appears in the forms of cormorant and toad, rather than anything impressive in power or grandeur, and also moral, since he is now a sly and envious eavesdropper rather than an imposing military leader. The epic voice warns us of Satan's emotions – 'inflamed with rage', 'his tumultuous breast', 'horror and doubt', 'hell within', 'despair', 'bitter memory', 'sad look', 'pale ire, envy and despair' – and then reminds us that 'heavenly minds from such distempers foul/Are ever clear' (IV. 9, 16, 18, 20, 23, 24, 28, 115, 118–19). Presumably we must understand that God's emotions, whether of anger or joviality, are not 'distempers' because they are 'just'.

Satan's speech echoes the invocation to Light at the start of the previous book, except that Satan addresses the sun to say 'how I hate thy beams' because they remind him of his previous condition in heaven (IV. 37). Satan, possibly as a result of Uriel's account of the creation at the end of Book III, now admits for the first time that he was created, and not 'self-begot' as he had argued during the War in Heaven (IV. 43; V. 860). Looking back, he feels it might have been no great hardship to have praised God, after all. His reasoning leads him to blame God, first for not making him a lower-ranking angel, in which case he would probably not have aspired to be 'highest', and second for his 'free love' which gave all creatures free will: 'Be then his love accursed, since love or hate,/To me alike, it deals eternal woe' (IV. 69–70). Whereas in his words to Beelzebub in Book I Satan had argued that 'the mind is its own place, and in itself/Can make a heaven of hell, and hell of heaven', his despair now is shown by his acknowledgement that 'which way I fly is hell; my self am hell' (I. 254–5; IV. 75). He finds the only way out of his present position to be submission, which, recalling his public role as leader of the fallen angels, would be shameful and therefore impossible. The conflict between his public persona before the fallen angels, who 'adore' him, and his private 'torments' is hard to bear: 'such joy ambition finds' (IV. 88, 89, 92). Anyway, he argues, having hated God so much, he could never be truly reconciled to him, and repentance would only lead to a 'worse relapse/And heavier fall' (IV. 100–101). This is the point of psychological analysis that God had made previously, in forecasting that those who refused to listen to conscience would 'hard be hardened, blind be blinded, more' (III. 200). Thus Satan reaches an impasse: submission to God is the only way out, but that would involve unthinkable shame before his followers, in addition to the likelihood of a further relapse. So his resolute conclusion is:

> *So farewell hope, and with hope farewell fear,*
> *Farewell remorse: all good to me is lost;*
> *Evil be thou my good; by thee at least*
> *Divided empire with heaven's king I hold.*
>
> (IV. 108–11)

He now turns towards Eden.

5 Adam and Eve in Paradise: IV. 131–775

'Paradise' is the name of the garden within the land of Eden. It is situated in an upland region round which grows an impassable wilderness covered by high trees. Above them is the wall of Paradise, giving a view of Eden, and higher than that grow fruit trees which, since there were no seasons before the Fall, bear 'blossoms and fruits at once' (IV. 148). The sweet 'native perfumes' of Paradise, which Milton, the blind poet, might be expected to emphasize, are vividly reinforced by epic similes, and the whole upward visual movement of the description is soon echoed by Satan's contemptuous leap over 'the undergrowth/Or shrubs and tangling bushes', so that he, like Superman, in a punning phrase, 'at one slight bound high over leaped all bound' (IV. 175–6, 181). But Milton likens him, not to a comic character, but to a wolf entering a sheep-pen, to a thief entering a house over the tiles, and to 'lewd hirelings' entering the church: Milton for many years had been against a salaried ministry. Satan sits like a cormorant, a bird symbolic of greed, on the tree of life (eating of the fruit of which was symbolic of gaining eternal life), 'devising death' (IV. 197).

Paradise is both literary and horticultural. Though Milton refers to other literary gardens such as the 'Hesperian gardens', the 'fair field of Enna', the 'sweet grove of Daphne', and 'Mount Amara' for negative comparison with his Paradise, he emphasizes the horticultural: he wants the reader to feel 'nature's whole wealth' exposed 'to all delight of human sense' (III. 568; IV. 250, 269, 273, 281, 206–7). Consider his description: the brooks ran with nectar which fed

Flowers worthy of Paradise which not nice art
In beds and curious knots, but nature boon
Poured forth profuse on hill and dale and plain,
Both where the morning sun first warmly smote
The open field, and where the unpierced shade
Embrowned the noontide bowers: thus was this place,
A happy rural seat of various view;
Groves whose rich trees wept odorous gums and balm,
Others whose fruit burnished with golden rind
Hung amiable, Hesperian fables true,
If true, here only, and of delicious taste:
Betwixt them lawns, or level downs, and flocks
Grazing the tender herb, were interposed,
Or palmy hillock, or the flowery lap
Of some irriguous valley spread her store,

Flowers of all hue, and without thorn the rose:
Another side, umbrageous grots and caves
Of cool recess, o'er which the mantling vine
Lays forth her purple grape, and gently creeps
Luxuriant; mean while murmuring waters fall
Down the slope hills, dispersed, or in a lake,
That to the fringed bank with myrtle crowned,
Her crystal mirror holds, unite their streams.
The birds their choir apply; airs, vernal airs,
Breathing the smell of field and grove, attune
The trembling leaves, while universal Pan
Knit with the Graces and the Hours in dance
Led on the eternal spring.

(IV. 241–68)

The contrast between 'nice [i.e. 'intricate'] art' and 'nature boon [i.e. 'bounteous']' reproduces an old argument which was very much alive in the seventeenth century.

John Evelyn, in his *Diary*, records a visit in 1644 to Cardinal Richelieu's estate at Reuil in central France. The gardens featured 'walks of vast lengths, so accurately kept and cultivated', symmetrical sections, and geometric regularity. The formality of French gardens in the seventeenth century was well known in England, and Charles II, while in exile in France prior to his restoration to the English throne in 1660, would doubtless have seen many examples. The gardens of Versailles, which began to be constructed in the 1660s, were only the climax of a French tradition to which English taste was hostile.[3] Gardens of geometric formality, constructed with 'nice art' rather than reflecting natural bounty, demonstrated a domination over nature, with political implications. For long, straight avenues directing the eye from palace windows to the furthest horizon, and vast artificial pools reflecting the palace, contrived to give the impression that the palace, and therefore its owner, was the centre of the universe. In fact, Louis XIV, who commissioned the gardens and palace at Versailles, became known as Roi Soleil, or Sun King. The French formal garden was implicitly autocratic. Milton's Paradise, on the other hand, can be seen in this context as essentially anti-French and anti-royalist, reflecting a belief in freedom constrained only by the limitations of reasoned restraint – the 'pleasant labour' of Adam and Eve (IV. 625). It is a 'happy rural seat of *various* view': an English country estate with natural, non-symmetrical variety, as the description makes clear. Paradise is watered with a natural fountain, drawn up by some sort of capillary action 'through veins/Of porous earth' (IV. 227–8), and there is no symmetry about the water movements, a lake mirroring only its 'fringed bank with myrtle crowned'. The description of Paradise appeals to all the senses, not just the visual: 'odorous', 'delicious taste', 'cool recess', 'murmuring waters' are examples. While the impression of harmony produced by the description is common to earlier ideal gardens, such as those in Tasso and Spenser, the pun on 'choir ... airs ... attune' with which this description ends is Milton's own. 'Airs' are breezes which carry the 'smell of field and grove', but they are also melodies which 'attune the trembling leaves'.

If Milton's Paradise can be seen to represent a position on one side of an argument between authoritarian control of nature and natural freedom and variety, his Adam and Eve show up the problems in his position with regard to the issue of authority versus freedom. This issue comes to a climax in Book IX when Adam and Eve blame each other for the Fall, so it is central to our understanding of the poem as a whole. It will first be necessary to look at some of the ramifications of 'freedom' and 'servitude' in the mid seventeenth century.

The Putney Debates in 1647 had addressed the issue of who should be eligible to vote in parliamentary elections. Both the army leaders, including Cromwell, and the Levellers, a radical group well represented among the soldiers, who campaigned against social distinctions and for 'levelling', agreed that only free men were entitled to vote. They further agreed that 'freedom' meant economic independence, that is, not being dependent on the will of an 'employer' for wages. Cromwell and the army leaders assumed that this meant owning freehold land or trading rights, whereas the Levellers, from their different class position, assumed that 'property in his own labour', or being self-employed, made a man free. Nevertheless, the concept of freedom was, for both groups, intimately connected with ideas of ownership and authority, and actually defined what made a man fully 'human'. freedom from the wills of others. Those who were not free from the wills of others in these ways, and who were thus not fully 'human', were servants and alms-takers. In the seventeenth century, the word 'servant' meant 'anyone who worked for an employer for wages', and was not narrowed in meaning as it is today.[4] 'In-servants' would include workers on the land or in industry (such as clothiers, craftsmen, etc.) who lived *in* the employer's household, which was usually also the place of work, and they would normally remain such until they became 'out-servants', by getting married and moving *out*. For political purposes, servants, it was agreed, should be 'included in their masters', or employers.[5] As far as women were concerned, Lilburne, the Leveller leader, wrote that man and woman were 'by nature all equal and alike in power, dignity, authority, and majesty, none of them having by nature any authority, dominion or magisterial power one over or above another' except 'by mutual agreement or consent'.[6] Despite this avowal of spiritual equality, however, he and the Levellers never claimed for women equal political rights with men. Like servants, they were apparently considered to be 'included in their masters'. This very contradiction, between an implied, or 'spiritual', equality and a practical inequality, is to be found reproduced in *Paradise Lost.*

Satan, convinced that it was 'better to reign in hell than *serve* in heaven', had, at the start of the War in Heaven, argued with the faithful seraph Abdiel about the relative merits of servitude in heaven and his own new-found freedom as a rebel. He feels that he has ceased being a sort of 'employee' of God's, and has, through his free enterprise, become somehow a 'free' and authentic person. Satan says:

> *At first I thought that liberty and heaven*
> *To heavenly souls had all been one; but now*
> *I see that most through sloth had rather serve,*
> *Ministering spirits, trained up in feast and song;*
> *Such hast thou armed, the minstrelsy of heaven,*
> *Servility with freedom to contend,*
> *As both their deeds compared this day shall prove.*
>
> (VI. 164–70)

Abdiel, however, makes a crucial distinction for our understanding of the issue of authority which is central to the poem:

> *Unjustly thou deprav'st it with the name*
> *Of servitude to serve whom God ordains,*
> *Or nature; God and nature bid the same,*
> *When he who rules is worthiest, and excels*
> *Them whom he governs. This is servitude,*
> *To serve the unwise, or him who hath rebelled*
> *Against his worthier, as thine now serve thee,*
> *Thy self not free, but to thy self enthralled.*
>
> (VI. 174–81)

Thus serving God, being his 'employee', is not servitude, but is like obeying nature: God's law is Natural Law. Serving God is true freedom, whereas serving the rebel or the unwise is true servitude, and places one in the control of the will of another.

In the description of Adam and Eve in Book IV we can now see the beginnings of the tension between freedom and servitude for Eve, which leads eventually to the Fall. On their first appearance (which is to the view of Satan) both Adam and Eve are described as 'lords of all' with 'looks divine', and both reflect the image of their maker 'in true filial freedom' (IV. 290–94). They walk 'hand in hand' and are 'linked in happy nuptial league', and Adam later addresses Eve as 'sole partner . . . of all these joys' (IV. 321, 339, 411). Thus their independence (freedom) and companionate equality are implied. On the other hand, they are explicitly 'not equal' (IV. 296). Adam's face declares 'absolute rule' ('absolute' here means 'unconditional', or 'unqualified by the wills of others', i.e. 'free', rather than 'despotic' or 'arbitrary' (IV. 301)). Eve is understood to be 'included in her master', or husband: 'He for God only, she for God in him' (IV. 299). Eve's subjection is symbolized by her hair, for whereas Adam's hair 'manly hung/Clustering', like bunches of grapes, Eve's longer hair was in 'wanton ringlets', like the *ancillary* 'tendrils' of the vine (VI. 302–3, 307–8). Further, in their emotional life, it was Eve who 'yielded with coy submission', a subservience that is reinforced only twenty-three lines later when the same word 'yielded' is used to describe the passive offering of fruit by the 'compliant boughs' (IV. 310, 333).

This tension between equality and submission reflects real conflicts within the experience of marriage that are specific to the seventeenth century. One historian of the period, Lawrence Stone, writes:

> The many legal, political and educational changes that took place in the late seventeenth and eighteenth centuries were largely consequences of changes in ideas about the nature of marital relations. The increasing stress laid by the early seventeenth-century preachers on the need for companionship in marriage in the long run tended to undercut their own arguments in favour of the maintenance of strict wifely subjection and obedience.[7]

Though other historians have quarrelled with Stone's location of this change in the nature of marital relations in the seventeenth century, and argued that the 'patriarchal' and 'companionate' types of marriage are 'poles of an enduring continuum of marital relations', nevertheless this issue is at the centre of the human interest of *Paradise Lost*.[8]

Milton's writings on divorce (he had published four pamphlets on the subject between 1643 and 1645) emphasize a new and radical attitude about what is really important in marriage. The orthodox view was in the *Book of Common Prayer*, which in 1549 had added to the two previous and widely accepted purposes of marriage a third one:

> First, it was ordained for the procreation of children, to be brought up in the fear and nurture of the Lord, and to the praise of his holy name.

> Secondly, it was ordained for a remedy against sin, and to avoid fornication, that such persons as have not the gift of continency, might marry, and keep themselves undefiled members of Christ's body.
>
> Thirdly, it was ordained for the mutual society, help, and comfort that the one ought to have of the other, both in prosperity and adversity.

Milton, however, argued strongly for a revised order of priorities, and, in his pamphlet *The Doctrine and Discipline of Divorce* (1643), he wrote:

> God in the first ordaining of marriage, taught us to what end he did it, in words expressly implying the apt and cheerfull conversation [i.e. 'companionship'] of man with woman, to comfort and refresh him against the evill of solitary life, not mentioning the purpose of generation till afterwards, as being but a secondary end in dignity, though not in necessity.[9]

As for avoidance of fornication, he argues, 'strict life and labour with the abatement of a full diet' may handle that adequately. The 'burning' which Paul refers to ('It is better to marry than to burn', I Corinthians 7:9) is, Milton claims, not a reference to uncontrollable lust, but to loneliness: 'the desire and longing to put off an unkindly solitarines by uniting another body, but not without a fit soule to his in the cheerfull society of wedlock'.[10]

Thus mutuality in marriage is significantly foregrounded in Milton's thought. Adam and Eve exist in 'happy nuptial league', to the envy of Satan, who desires 'league .../And mutual amity' with them, and is tormented by the sight of them 'imparadised in one another's arms' (IV. 339, 375–6, 506). The recriminations after the Fall centre on the extent to which the mutuality of the married couple has undermined Adam's authority as husband.

Adam and Eve, though naked, are 'with native honour clad', and Milton thus avoids the simple identification of 'honour' with the restricting and distorting forms of civilized life: those he calls 'honour dishonourable, /Sin-bred' (IV. 289, 314–15). This first description of Adam and Eve contains resonances that echo through the whole poem and remind us ominously of what is to come. Here the couple go 'hand in hand': just before the Fall, in Book IX, Eve withdraws 'from her husband's hand her hand', and, finally, at the end of the poem, they walk through Eden 'hand in hand with wandering steps and slow' to start the course of human history (IV. 321; IX. 385; XII. 648). Here their work is 'sweet gardening labour', just enough to make 'ease/More easy'; Adam's curse later decrees that 'in the sweat of thy face shalt thou eat bread', and the word 'labour' after the Fall comes to mean hard labour, associated with sweat (IV. 328–30; X. 205; XI. 172). Similarly, the reference here to the 'fruits' which satisfy their appetite echoes the first line of the poem – 'the fruit/Of that forbidden tree' – and also anticipates the centrality of 'fruit' to the Fall in Book IX, in which book alone there are thirty-two references to fruit and its derivatives (fruits, fruitless), compared with only sixty-one in the whole of the rest of the poem.

As evening approaches, Satan observes the couple with another emotional soliloquy. His mission requires him to secure an alliance with Adam and Eve in defiance of God: this is his 'public reason just/Honour and empire with revenge enlarged' (IV. 389–90). Yet in other circumstances he 'could love' the pair, 'could pity' them and 'melt' at their 'harmless innocence' (IV. 363, 374, 388–9). He would 'abhor' what he is about to do, were it not for the overriding compulsion of his public role. Given his position as leader of hell's angels, he feels hospitable to the happy couple – 'hell shall unfold,/And send forth all her kings' (IV. 381–3) – and if hell is not Paradise, that is the fault of its maker, he argues. It seems now to be with reluctance that his revenge involves Adam and Eve, and in this we may regard Satan as sincere. He is caught on the dilemma of the distinction between obligations of statesmanship and the impulse towards mutuality. It is this 'necessity' which, the epic voice comments, is the plea of tyrants and Satan's excuse for 'devilish deeds' (IV. 393–4). Satan now impersonates the shapes of various animals, which, after the Fall, became beasts of prey, such as the lion and tiger, as he metaphorically prepares to pounce.

Adam's first speech to Eve lovingly explains the power structure in which they live (IV. 411–39). God must be good since he created them and their 'ample world' with no obligation to do so, and with no expectation of reward. He merely requires one symbolic act of obedience, insignificant among 'so many signs of power and rule' that he has conferred upon them, and that is that they do not eat of the 'tree/Of knowledge' (IV. 429, 423–4). The eavesdropping Satan is thus given the clue he is looking for, their potential weak spot. Adam urges Eve not to 'think hard/One easy prohibition', and suggests that they follow their 'delightful task/To prune these growing plants, and tend these flowers,/Which, were it toilsome, yet with thee were sweet' (IV. 432–3, 437–9). Milton thus ensures that Adam and Eve *work* in Paradise, and he gives the old maxim *laborare est orare* (to work is to worship) an intenser significance. The puritan saw labour not as a punishment for the Fall: the latter merely changed its nature. Labour was for the puritan a spiritual end in itself, an idealized form of worship, rather than a mere material necessity.[11] Labour, or work, is itself a prerequisite for the holy life, and this accounts for Milton's rejection of the languorous self-indulgence depicted in many previous accounts of

Paradise, or the Golden Age. Farm work in the seventeenth century was, in fact, normally a collaborative effort between husband and wife: one historian writes, 'the male and female spheres, though largely separate, overlapped ... between the farmer and his wife there had to be complete mutual trust and confidence'.[12]

Eve replies to Adam, whom she acknowledges as her 'guide/And head', in terms of self-subjection: she is the happier of the pair because she can enjoy Adam, who is 'pre-eminent by so much odds', whereas he only has her (IV. 442–3, 447). She describes the day of her creation, which anticipates her susceptibility to flattery which leads to the Fall. On first achieving consciousness she fell in love with her own reflection in a lake, and would, like Narcissus, have pined away for love of herself had not a voice led her to Adam, whose 'image' it said she was (IV. 472).[13] At first she turned away, thinking him less attractive than her own image, but he recalled her with the words:

Whom fly'st thou? Whom thou fly'st, of him thou art,
His flesh, his bone; to give thee being I lent
Out of my side to thee, nearest my heart
Substantial life, to have thee by my side
Henceforth an individual solace dear;
Part of my soul I seek thee, and thee claim
My other half.

(IV. 482–8)

Here we see expressed the claims for Adam's authority over Eve: he gave her being, and she is therefore part of his soul. But there is also an intimation of their equality: she is his other *half*, and it was commonplace, since at least the early fifteenth century, to observe that Eve was made of Adam's *rib* in order that she be his companion, 'not of his foot to be his thrall [i.e. 'slave'], nor his head to be his master'.[14] With that, Eve continues,

... thy gentle hand
Seized mine, I yielded, and from that time see
How beauty is excelled by manly grace
And wisdom, which alone is truly fair.

(IV. 488–91)

Adam's seizing of Eve's hand here for the first time is an anticipation of the moment after the Fall when 'her hand he seized' and they make love as 'solace of their sin' (IX. 1037, 1044). They now kiss, and the vocabulary produces an atmosphere of fecundity: 'swelling breast', 'impregns the clouds', 'matron lip' (IV. 495, 500, 501).

Satan hates it. From this point his attitude to Adam and Eve is shown as motivated by malice. Satan had taken a mistress in heaven, called Sin, but in hell no sex-life is allowed, and instead the devils are tormented with 'fierce desire' (II. 765–7; IV. 509). Thus the sight of Adam and Eve 'imparadised in one another's arms/The happier Eden' goads him into a destructive plan based on the information gained from his eavesdropping (IV.506–7, 423). He will 'excite their minds/With more desire to know' (IV. 522–3). Since knowledge is power, this will represent a threat, and might make them 'equal with gods': 'aspiring to be such,/They taste and die: what likelier can ensue?' (IV. 526–7). He turns away with seeming relish for the brevity of their pleasures which he finds so unbearable. His political objectives have disappeared from his mind: his motives now seem purely personal and vengeful against Adam and Eve, rather than even against God.

The scene switches briefly to heaven, where it is now sunset, Paradise-time. Gabriel, on guard over Paradise, is approached by Uriel in great haste, who recounts his meeting at noon with the 'stripling cherub', Satan (III. 636). He tells how he directed him to earth in good faith, but then, noticing that his looks when he first landed were 'with passions foul obscured', realized that he was probably a fallen angel (IV. 118, 571). We know, of course, that God has already announced, not only that Satan was on his way to earth, but that the Fall would occur as a result: nevertheless, Gabriel promises to investigate the suspected break-in (III. 86–95). Milton now, in a passage of consummate brilliance, returns the scene to earth with a description of evening. The sun has set 'beneath the Azores', and Milton avoids choosing between the old Ptolemaic view of the universe with the earth at the centre, and the Copernican view which was sun-centred:

> *... whether the bright orb,*
> *Incredible how swift, had thither rolled*
> *Diurnal, or this less voluble* [i.e. 'apt to rotate'] *earth*
> *By shorter flight to the east, had left him there*
> *Arraying with reflected purple and gold*
> *The clouds that on his western throne attend:*
> *Now came still evening on, and twilight grey*
> *Had in her sober livery all things clad;*
> *Silence accompanied, for beast and bird,*
> *They to their grassy couch, these to their nests*

Were slunk, all but the wakeful nightingale;
She all night long her amorous descant sung;
Silence was pleased: now glowed the firmament
With living sapphires: Hesperus that led
The starry host, rode brightest, till the moon
Rising in clouded majesty, at length
Apparent queen unveiled her peerless light,
And o'er the dark her silver mantle threw.

(IV. 592–609)

One argument in favour of the Copernican system is glanced at in the phrase 'incredible how swift': under the Ptolemaic system, the sun would need to travel at enormous, in fact astronomical, speed if it were to travel daily round the earth. But the passage submerges this argument in a striking sequence of images of regal decorum and dress, in which the kingly sun, associated with purple and gold, gives way to the sober grey livery of evening, to be followed by the starry host, and then the 'apparent queen', the moon, with her silver mantle.

Adam now addresses Eve as 'fair consort', thus echoing the regal imagery of the sun and moon just preceding (IV. 610). He explains to Eve that, for humans, labour and rest are analogous to day and night, and that they must be up before dawn at their 'pleasant labour', which consists of trimming back and tidying up the luxuriant vegetation in Paradise (IV. 625). Eve responds with submissive formality, addressing him as 'my author and disposer', and then speaks one of the most beautiful love-lyrics in all seventeenth-century poetry:

With thee conversing I forget all time,
All seasons and their change, all please alike.
Sweet is the breath of morn, her rising sweet,
With charm of earliest birds; pleasant the sun
When first on this delightful land he spreads
His orient beams, on herb, tree, fruit, and flower,
Glistering with dew; fragrant the fertile earth
After soft showers; and sweet the coming on
Of grateful evening mild, then silent night
With this her solemn bird and this fair moon,
And these the gems of heaven, her starry train:
But neither breath of morn when she ascends
With charm of earliest birds, nor rising sun
On this delightful land, nor herb, fruit, flower,
Glistering with dew, nor fragrance after showers,
Nor grateful evening mild, nor silent night

With this her solemn bird, nor walk by moon,
Or glittering starlight without thee is sweet.

(IV. 639–56)

The formal symmetry, in which the first half is echoed with variations by the second in negatives, gives this lyric a shape which is wonderfully impressive as a statement of wholeness, of emotional commitment, and of innocent love.

The couple now move 'hand in hand' to their 'blissful bower', which becomes an emblem of true married love (IV. 689–90). Adam ends the day in a simple prayer of thanks to God, delighting in 'our mutual help/And mutual love, the crown of all our bliss/Ordained by thee', and then 'into their inmost bower/Handed [i.e. 'hand in hand'] they went' (IV. 727–9, 738–9). Milton makes it absolutely clear that they make love before the Fall, which had been a point of theological contention, since, if this is accepted, there was a possibility that Eve might have conceived a sinless child. But, in his panegyric on married love, Milton is more concerned to intervene in an argument over sexuality. The general view of the early Church fathers, such as St Jerome, was that all sex was unclean. The Reformation had introduced the concept of *holy* matrimony, but in the seventeenth century the consensus of theological opinion emphasized the idea of 'matrimonial chastity', which meant moderation of sexual relations even inside marriage.[15] Milton, however, here confirms and defends the importance of 'connubial' or 'wedded love', which the epic voice describes as 'mysterious', in the sense of a 'mystery', or symbol of the union between Christ and his Church (IV. 743, 750). To understand 'purity' and 'innocence' as virginity is hypocrisy, it is argued. Wedded love does not, however, mean immoderate passion or promiscuity: it is the only thing in Paradise which is private, and, because the sexual relation is seen here as the *result* of love rather than its cause, it is superior to the sophisticated amours of court, or loveless relations with harlots (IV. 752, 766–7). Wedded love in Paradise is, in fact, 'founded in reason', and Milton had argued the reasons for the importance of marriage at length in his divorce pamphlets nearly twenty years earlier. At this point in the poem they are, however, curtailed by these poignant lines:

These lulled by the nightingales embracing slept,
And on their naked limbs the flowery roof
Showered roses, which the morn repaired. Sleep on
Blest pair; and O yet happiest if ye seek
No happier state, and know to know no more.

(IV. 771–5)

Thus passes their last night of innocent love. The rose was a common symbol of the transience of human happiness: in Book IX we later see Eve supporting the drooping heads of roses just prior to her temptation (IX. 426–30). But it is the paradox of knowledge which is crucial: for them as for us, to 'know to know no more' is not a realistic possibility.

6 Satan's Arrest: IV. 776–1015

With Adam and Eve asleep, the scene turns now to heaven, where Gabriel is sending out search-parties for the intruder. Ithuriel and Zephon, minor angels, discover him 'squat like a toad, close at the ear of Eve', where he is attempting to influence her unconscious and raise 'distempered, discontented thoughts,/Vain hopes, vain aims, inordinate desires/Blown up with high conceits engendering pride' (IV. 800, 807–9). This creature must clearly be the intruder, since no 'beast, bird, insect, or worm' was allowed in the blissful bower (IV. 704). When Ithuriel touches the toad with his spear, the 'celestial temper', both of the spear in the sense of 'alloy', and of Ithuriel in the sense of 'temperament', causes Satan to return explosively to his own likeness (IV. 813). Asked who he is and what he is doing, Satan replies with magisterial scorn, 'Not to know me argues your selves unknown,/The lowest of your throng' (IV. 831–2). Zephon, undismayed, informs Satan that since his rebellion he has lost his former glory and has taken on the dark characteristics of hell. Satan, though abashed before the 'severe ... youthful beauty' and virtue of the cherubs, again puts on a public face, and demands to be taken to their leader, refusing to deal with the lower ranks (IV. 845). He still appears haughty, 'like a proud steed', though reined, because in his heart he is awe-struck by the presence of goodness (IV. 858, 860).

Satan is taken to Gabriel, who recognizes him at once in his 'faded splendour wan', and immediately with a stern look demands to know what he has been doing in forbidden territory (IV. 870). Silly question, replies Satan: I was trying to escape from my pain, and if God had intended me to stay in hell he would have made the gates more secure. But, Gabriel replies, it's silly to expect to escape pain by provoking God's infinite anger, and anyway why wasn't it that 'all hell broke loose' when you escaped from your pain, 'courageous chief' (IV. 918, 920)? Satan, insulted, returns the gibe: a faithful leader doesn't risk all his troops until he has spied out the territory, but what would Gabriel and his showy legions know about military strategy, being more practised at cringing before God's throne than at fighting? Ah, replies Gabriel, having caught

Satan in a lie, you pretend to be escaping from pain, but then admit to spying, so how can you call yourself a 'faithful' leader? And you pretend to be 'patron of liberty', but none fawned and cringed more than you before God, and only in order to 'dispossess him, and thy self to reign' (IV. 958, 961). Get to hell out of here, or I'll drag you in there in chains! Enraged, Satan warns, capture me first, but expect to feel 'my prevailing arm', whatever your protection (IV. 973)!

The bitter row between Gabriel and Satan ends in awesome confrontation: the angelic squadrons close in like a restless field of corn, while Satan swells up to an immense stature, like the mountains Teneriff or Atlas, whose tops reputedly reached the sky (IV. 987). (Atlas also in mythology was a Titan, a rebel against the divine authority.) At this point, we are informed, what is at risk is not only Paradise, but the whole created universe (IV. 991–5). God then intervenes and displays in the heavens his 'golden scales', which we might identify with the constellation Libra, the seventh sign of the Zodiac (IV. 997). He judges the results 'of parting and of fight', and parting has the greater weight (IV.1003). Gabriel interprets this to mean that Satan would be 'light', i.e. the loser, in a fight, and possibly Satan takes it to mean the same. But from God's point of view, fighting would mean the defeat of Satan, and therefore that Adam and Eve's obedience would be untested. Is God here again desperately manipulating events to ensure that the Fall actually occurs, by making certain that Satan, who has already escaped from hell, and managed to enter Paradise, and then been captured, is allowed yet again to get away?[16] Certainly the whole apparatus of divine guards and infantry seems merely a façade which, when tested, proves worthless: but that was one of the insoluble narrative problems that Milton faced in attempting to dramatize omnipotence. Satan therefore withdraws, at midnight; and we look forward to the next day with some anticipation to discover the effects of his work as 'a toad, close at the ear of Eve' (IV. 800).

IV The Third Day: Paradise – the Lunch-Party Conversation

1 Eve's Dream: V. 1–223

Adam wakes at first light and softly wakes Eve, who has slept badly. She tells him of the dream which has left her disturbed: a voice that she thought at first was Adam's close at her ear seemed to wake her and flatter her with the cadences of gallantry. She rose and walked to the tree of knowledge, where an angel-like figure appeared and addressed the tree. He queried the justice of the ban on eating the fruit, and then ate of it himself and invited her to eat also, so that she might become a goddess and 'as we, sometimes/Ascend to heaven' (V. 79–80). He held the fruit to her mouth, which stirred her appetite so that she felt she must taste it. Then quickly she was aloft with him, looking down on the earth – and suddenly was alone and asleep. In this dream we can see the ominous anticipation of the Fall in Book IX. Compare, for example, these words to Eve:

Whom to behold but thee, nature's desire,
In whose sight all things joy, with ravishment
Attracted by thy beauty still to gaze.

(V. 45–7)

with these:

Thee all things living gaze on, all things thine
By gift, and thy celestial beauty adore
With ravishment beheld.

(IX. 539–41)

or compare these words to the tree:

Deigns none to ease thy load and taste thy sweet,
Nor God, nor man; is knowledge so despised?
Or envy, or what reserve forbids to taste?

(V. 59–61)

with these words to Eve:

. . . And wherein lies
The offence, that man should thus attain to know?
What can your knowledge hurt him, or this tree

Impart against his will if all be his?
Or is it envy, and can envy dwell
In heavenly breasts?

(IX. 725–30)

Adam, on being told of this dream, wrestles with the problem of the origin of evil. If having a sinful dream makes Eve a sinner, then this was the moment of her real fall from innocence to sin. Adam reasons that this was not the case, in accordance with seventeenth-century psychology. 'Fancy' is the faculty which forms 'airy shapes' from material provided by the five senses, but it is subordinate to reason, which is the chief faculty and 'frames/All what we affirm or what deny, and call/Our knowledge or opinion' (V. 105–8). When reason is absent, however, as in dreams, fancy can go wild, but if evil comes and goes in such circumstances, 'unapproved' by the intellect, no blame can be attached to the dreamer. Should reason be subordinated to a lesser faculty in any other circumstances, of course, as a result of pride or vanity, for example, the implications and outcome would be quite different. Eve at this point is cheered, though she nevertheless weeps the first tears in Paradise.

Ready for work, Adam and Eve fall to a spontaneously eloquent morning prayer on the sight of Paradise in the light of the rising sun, and this brings peace and calm to their thoughts:

Ye mists and exhalations that now rise
From hill or steaming lake, dusky or grey,
Till the sun paint your fleecy skirts with gold,
In honour to the world's great author rise,
Whether to deck with clouds the uncoloured sky,
Or wet the thirsty earth with falling showers,
Rising or falling still advance his praise.

(V. 185–91)

They set off for work, and their gardening is described in the imagery of marriage, symbolic of their new union following their prayer together:

. . . they led the vine
To wed her elm; she spoused about him twines
Her marriageable arms, and with her brings
Her dower the adopted clusters, to adorn
His barren leaves.

(V. 215–19)

2 Raphael's Arrival and Advice: V. 224–560

The poignancy of this happy union between Adam and Eve, which we know will prove so temporary in its present form, even strikes God, who now feels the emotion of 'pity' for them. He therefore instructs Raphael to go down and converse with Adam, in order to emphasize to him that he has free will, and to warn him of 'his danger, and from whom', so that Adam will not be able to claim that he was 'unadmonished, unforewarned' if he wilfully disobeys (V. 239, 245). Yet again we see here Milton's narrative problem: God has already foreseen that Adam will transgress, but here motivated by pity instructs that he be warned, knowing the warning must be useless. Likewise, Raphael's warning when it comes makes no mention of the capture of Satan in Eden, which God had told him about (V. 224–8). Is this because this very pertinent fact might have made Adam too wary to transgress, and thus hindered the demands of the narrative? This problem, as we have already shown, results directly from attempting to make omnipotence and omniscience speak, feel, and act as a person.

Raphael flies straight to earth, passing on his way 'worlds and worlds', and arrives at the eastern edge of Paradise where the gate is, in contrast with Satan's earlier illegal entry (V. 268, 275; IV. 178, 181). He reassumes his appearance as a glorious six-winged seraph, and approaches Adam and Eve. Adam is sitting in the shade at the door of their bower, as it is about noon, and Eve is inside preparing food. On seeing Raphael, Adam immediately calls to Eve and asks her to prepare a generous feast, and Eve at once rushes out to pick the very best fresh food. It is of note here that Eve, in this domestic scene, for the first time calls her husband Adam, and abandons the formality of her previous addresses. Partly this might be because she makes a pun on the meaning of 'Adam', which supposedly in Hebrew meant 'red' in reference to the red earth out of which he was made, when she says 'Adam, earth's hallowed mould' (V. 321); but it also reveals a position in relation to an issue for debate in the later seventeenth century. Lawrence Stone comments:

> Around 1700 this issue of what to call a husband was clearly a widely debated issue, the conservatives realizing the egalitarian and anti-patriarchal implications of a change to the use of the first name by a wife to a husband.[1]

Eve, like a good hostess, plans a well-balanced meal, though there is no cooking involved, since fire was given to mankind as evidence of God's mercy after the Fall (X. 1078–81). Eve's 'taste' is here unfallen as she considers:

What choice to choose for delicacy best,
What order, so contrived as not to mix
Tastes, not well joined, inelegant, but bring
Taste after taste upheld with kindliest change.

(V. 333–6)

This passage takes its place in the pattern of references to 'taste' which permeates *Paradise Lost*, from the second line of the poem, through the emphasis on taste in Eve's dream, to the lines of Adam after the Fall which seem to make a sick parody of the present passage ('Eve, now I see thou art exact of taste/And elegant' (IX. 1017–18)). Their drink consists of unfermented grape-juice ('inoffensive must'), since intoxication, with its loss of rational control, was unknown prior to the Fall. Adam, meanwhile, greets Raphael and invites him to lunch. Milton emphasizes that Adam's nakedness gives him more dignity before his 'godlike guest' than all the 'tedious pomp that waits/On princes', and Eve similarly is 'undecked' and 'more lovely fair' than imaginary goddesses (V. 351–5, 380). But here occurs a curious double meaning, in the words 'no veil/She needed, *virtue-proof*, no thought infirm/Altered her cheek' (V. 383–5). The dominant meaning seems to be that Eve's virtue is her protection, but since Raphael is referred to thirteen lines previously as 'the angelic virtue', then, by analogy with words like 'waterproof' or 'fireproof', the word might imply secondarily, and again ominously, that Eve is impervious to Raphael.

Eating is now the first topic of conversation. Adam's possible blunder in offering material food to an angel prompts him to make oblique enquiries about the nature of angels. Milton's angels *eat*: they do not merely swallow, but actually digest, and in this view of them Milton sides with the Platonic theologians against the old-fashioned Scholastic theologians, such as Thomas Aquinas, who believed angels to be non-material:

... So down they sat
And to their viands fell, nor seemingly
The angel, nor in mist, the common gloss
Of theologians, but with keen despatch
Of real hunger.

(V. 433–7)

This scene, of humans eating with an angel, reminds us that Adam and Eve already could enjoy communion with gods, and therefore of the pointlessness of eating the forbidden fruit to become like gods. The poem is thus centrally about 'eating', and Raphael makes it a principle which explains the interrelation of the whole universe, inanimate as well as animate:

> *For know, whatever was created, needs*
> *To be sustained and fed; of elements*
> *The grosser feeds the purer, earth the sea,*
> *Earth and the sea feed air . . .*
> *The sun that light imparts to all, receives*
> *From all his alimental recompense*
> *In humid exhalations.*
>
> (V. 414–17, 423–5)

Thus a harmonious world is metaphorically structured.

Adam in his desire 'to know' now warily begins to question Raphael about a variety of topics (V. 454). Raphael emphasizes the unity of all creation, which consists of 'one first matter all,/Indued with various forms', but which, like a plant, has roots, stalk, leaves, and flower with a fragrance analogous to spirits (V. 472–3, 484). He also distinguishes two sorts of reasoning:

> *Discursive, or intuitive; discourse*
> *Is oftest yours, the latter most is ours,*
> *Differing but in degree, of kind the same.*
>
> (V. 488–90)

Though angels and humans can use both forms, the discursive form of methodical reasoning is usually used by humans, whereas intuitive comprehension is naturally used by angels. We remember the fallen angels in Book II who had apparently lost their faculty of intuition, and were lost 'in wandering mazes' of discursive reasoning (II. 561).

Now Raphael comes to the purpose of his visit, reminding Adam of the importance of obedience if he wishes to remain happy, or even graduate to an ethereal state, like angels. Adam finds even the thought of disobedience absurd, but Raphael warns him to be careful:

> *God made thee perfect, not immutable;*
> *And good he made thee, but to persevere*
> *He left it in thy power, ordained thy will*
> *By nature free, not overruled by fate*
> *Inextricable, or strict necessity.*
>
> (V. 524–8)

Milton came to conceive of the relationship between freedom and obedience as quite straightforward: true freedom was doing of your own free will what ought to be done anyway, since 'God and nature bid the same' (VI. 176). To freedom he opposed the concept of 'licence', which meant self-indulgence, and was a form of slavery to the self. Satan is specifically accused of this later in the poem by Abdiel ('Thy self not free, but to thy self enthralled' (VI. 181), and Milton's Sonnet XII, written in 1646, attacks those who

> *... bawl for freedom in their senseless mood,*
> *And still revolt when truth would set them free.*
> *Licence they mean when they cry liberty;*
> *For who loves that, must first be wise and good.*

'Goodness' depends on 'wisdom', or reasoning correctly to make the right choices, and both are preconditions for true liberty. In his 1649 pamphlet *The Tenure of Kings and Magistrates*, Milton argued this point in a political context:

> For indeed none can love freedom heartilie, but good men; the rest love not freedom, but licence; which never hath more scope or more indulgence than under Tyrants.[2]

Augustine had explained the paradox of freedom in this way in the fourth century A.D.:

> Obedience is in a way the mother and guardian of all the other virtues in a rational creature, seeing that the rational creation has been so made that it is to man's advantage to be in subjection to God, and calamitous for him to act according to his own will, and not to obey the will of his Creator.[3]

Raphael now reveals to Adam that 'some are fallen, to disobedience fallen' already, and this excites Adam's curiosity yet further.

3 Raphael's Account of the Exaltation of the Son and the Council of War: V. 561–907

Raphael proceeds to relate the full story of recent events in heaven, starting with the following observation:

> *... what surmounts the reach*
> *Of human sense, I shall delineate so,*
> *By likening spiritual to corporal forms,*
> *As may express them best, though what if earth*
> *Be but the shadow of heaven, and things therein*
> *Each to other like, more than on earth is thought?*
>
> (V. 571–6)

Thus we as readers are challenged to interpret and demythologize the poem.

Raphael's narrative slips back to a time before creation, when 'Chaos wild/Reigned where these heavens [i.e. the astronomical heavens] now roll, where earth now rests' (V. 577–8). God summons all the angels to appear before him in a magnificent assembly, and then utters these fateful words:

> *Hear all ye angels, progeny of light,*
> *Thrones, dominations, princedoms, virtues, powers,*
> *Hear my decree, which unrevoked shall stand.*
> *This day I have begot whom I declare*
> *My only Son, and on this holy hill*
> *Him have anointed, whom ye now behold*
> *At my right hand; your head I him appoint;*
> *And by my self have sworn to him shall bow*
> *All knees in heaven, and shall confess him lord.*
>
> (V. 600–608)

This is the exaltation of the Son, which, as God foresees, causes Satan's rebellion. Since it is later made clear that God created everything, including the angels, through the agency of the Son, this moment, in the presence of the assembled angels, cannot be the 'birth' of the Son. Rather it paraphrases Psalm 2:7, and indicates God's honouring, or exalting, of the Son – in effect his coronation (V. 835–7). It is probably to be distinguished from the later exaltation forecast in Book III, which is to occur after the Son has come to earth (III. 313–29). There was a seventeenth-century tradition that this arbitrary act of the exaltation prompted Satan's rebellion, though there is no biblical evidence for making this connection.

Raphael's picture of life in heaven is exotic and idyllic. In the evening (there is day and night in heaven 'for change delectable, not need') a banquet is set up where all 'in communion sweet/Quaff immortality and joy' (V. 629, 637–8). At night all except God sleep, or sing melodious hymns, and are 'fanned with cool winds' in 'pavilions numberless' by 'living streams among the trees of life' (V. 652–5). Satan, however, is overcome with envy and malice and, unable to sleep, wakes Beelzebub at midnight and tells him to assemble their followers to leave before daybreak. The ostensible reason, clearly a lie, is to 'prepare/Fit entertainment to receive our king' (V. 689–90). One third of the angels obey him.

God, smiling, now makes an extraordinary speech to the Son:

Nearly it now concerns us to be sure
Of our omnipotence, and with what arms
We mean to hold what anciently we claim
Of deity or empire . . .
Let us advise, and to this hazard draw
With speed what force is left, and all employ
In our defence, lest unawares we lose
This our high place, our sanctuary, our hill.

(V. 721–32)

Is God pretending, as an in-joke with the Son, that his omnipotence is uncertain, and that his power rests merely on an 'ancient claim'? Is any 'hazard', or chance, really involved? Is therefore the whole impending war a sham, to make Satan and the rebels believe they have a chance to win, through a strategy on God's part of pretended weakness? If so, as William Empson argues, the joke is 'appallingly malignant'.[4] On the other hand, the narrative allows God little choice, since to have destroyed the rebels earlier would have been to deny their freedom, and to have done nothing would have been an abdication of his omnipotence. So we are again forced to the conclusion that the concept of benevolent omnipotence is incompatible with the narrative, and justifying the ways of God to men in a poem is more difficult than might have been expected for reasons that are literary as well as theological. The Son matches God's tone with a pun on 'dextrous' ('Know whether I be dextrous to subdue/Thy rebels'), where the word refers both to his sitting at God's 'right hand', and to his 'skilfulness' in battle (V. 741–2; VI. 892).

Satan meanwhile, returning to his impressive palace in the north, addresses his followers. Echoing the start of God's address, 'Thrones, dominations, princedoms, virtues, powers', he produces a magnificent piece of rhetoric, where one idea leads to another in one long dramatic sentence of thirteen lines, and climaxes in:

Will ye submit your necks, and choose to bend
The supple knee? Ye will not, if I trust
To know ye right, or if ye know your selves
Natives and sons of heaven possessed before
By none, and if not equal all, yet free,
Equally free; for orders and degrees
Jar not with liberty, but well consist.

(V. 787–93)

He continues, arguing that the free angels 'without law/Err not', and that they were 'ordained to govern, not to serve'. This is a persuasive argument: Milton, in his anti-monarchist pamphlet *The Tenure of Kings and Magistrates* (1649), had used similar arguments ('men naturally were born free' and were 'born to command and not to obey' until, following Adam's transgression, it was 'needfull to ordaine som authoritee') to lead to the conclusion that it is the 'liberty and right of free born Men, to be govern'd as seems to them best'.[5] Satan's speech also resembles the position of a medieval baron, whose allegiance to the throne depends on having some control over it. His argument in this view is therefore not with God himself so much as with the requirement for 'adoration' which the exaltation of the Son has imposed on the angels (V. 800).

Perhaps at this point Raphael's verbatim account of Satan's arguments is in danger of persuading Adam that he may be right. Anyway, the seraph Abdiel erupts in explosive opposition. 'Shalt thou give law to God,' he exclaims, 'shalt thou dispute/With him the points of liberty, who made/Thee what thou art?' (V. 822–4). Then, further, he refers to the Son 'by whom/As by his Word the mighty Father made all things, even thee' (V. 835–7). This comes as a profound shock to Satan, a stunning revelation, which he refuses to accept:

> *That we were formed then say'st thou? And the work*
> *Of secondary hands, by task transferred*
> *From Father to his Son? Strange point and new!*
> *Doctrine which we would know whence learned: who saw*
> *When this creation was? Remember'st thou*
> *Thy making, while the maker gave thee being?*
> *We know no time when we were not as now;*
> *Know none before us, self-begot, self-raised*
> *By our own quickening power . . .*
> *Our puissance is our own, our own right hand*
> *Shall teach us highest deeds, by proof to try*
> *Who is our equal: then thou shalt behold*
> *Whether by supplication we intend*
> *Address, and to begirt the almighty throne*
> *Beseeching or besieging.*
>
> (V. 853–69)

The verbal play on the last words shows Satan's proud confidence in his autonomy. He refuses to believe that he was created, let alone by the agency of the newly exalted Son. The moment that he does come to accept this, which is in his first soliloquy on earth as he approaches Paradise, is the turning-point in his career, when he sinks into increasing degeneracy in contrast with his previous imposing presence (IV. 43).

The sense that we might individually be somehow 'independent' or autonomous is a persistent human illusion, and one which provides another dimension to Milton's story. Augustine in his *City of God* uses religious terminology to say what existentialists, ecologists, socialists, and others might say with different terminology: it is sheer destructive folly to behave as if we were not 'contingent' and dependent on others and on nature for our being. This is Satan's folly, and this is how Augustine put it:

> To abandon God and to exist in oneself, that is to please oneself, is not immediately to lose all being; but it is to come nearer to nothingness. [Adam and Eve] would have been better able to be like gods if they had in obedience adhered to the supreme and real ground of their being, if they had not in pride made themselves their own ground. For created gods are gods not in their own true nature but by participation in the true God. By aiming at more, a man is diminished, when he elects to be self-sufficient and defects from the one who is really sufficient for him.[6]

We can at this point, then, both respond to Satan's splendid resistance and recognize its folly.

Abdiel gives his parting warning:

> *... I see thy fall*
> *Determined ...*
> *... Soon expect to feel*
> *His thunder on thy head, devouring fire.*
> *Then who created thee lamenting learn,*
> *When who can uncreate thee thou shalt know.*
>
> (V. 878–95)

Perhaps we can see in Raphael's description of Abdiel a self-description of Milton. Though the English people had apparently let God down, a failure which resulted in the disintegration of the Commonwealth and was to lead eventually to the Restoration of the monarchy, Milton kept his lonely faith, as did Abdiel, and gave his testimony, refusing all compromise in the face of 'hostile scorn', and fearless of violence:

> *So spake the seraph Abdiel faithful found,*
> *Among the faithless, faithful only he;*
> *Among innumerable false, unmoved,*
> *Unshaken, unseduced, unterrified*
> *His loyalty he kept, his love, his zeal;*

Nor number, nor example with him wrought
To swerve from truth, or change his constant mind
Though single. From amidst them forth he passed,
Long way through hostile scorn, which he sustained
Superior, nor of violence feared aught;
And with retorted scorn his back he turned
On those proud towers to swift destruction doomed.

(V. 896–907)

4 Raphael's Account of the War in Heaven: VI. 1–912

On Abdiel's return to heaven he finds war already in preparation, since his 'news' was already known (VI. 20). He is congratulated by God for his stand, essentially Milton's own stand:

Servant of God, well done, well hast thou fought
The better fight, who single hast maintained
Against revolted multitudes the cause
Of truth, in word mightier than they in arms;
And for the testimony of truth hast borne
Universal reproach, far worse to bear
Than violence.

(VI. 29–35)

Again in this book Milton faces a series of huge problems. One is that, though epics have traditionally centred on accounts of combat, battles, and wars, these accounts have been exciting because of the uncertainty or unexpectedness of the outcome: here, on the other hand, the outcome is certain. Since we know God must win, why is a three-day war necessary? (This is our old problem of how omnipotence either destroys the narrative by removing the uncertainty, or God's character by making him seem malicious.) A second problem is that, since angels cannot die, what is the point of a war with artillery and cannon (I. 117)? And a third is that, since Raphael is explaining what has happened in heaven 'by likening spiritual to corporal forms', how can this make any sense to the newly created Adam and Eve, who can have no conception of warfare?

One partial answer to all these problems could be that Milton is highlighting to his readers, rather than to Adam and Eve, the ultimate pointlessness of war. In 1648 he had written a sonnet in praise of General Fairfax, Commander-in-Chief of the New Model Army, who had laid siege to, and was soon to take, Colchester from the Royalists. The sonnet included these lines:

> *O yet a nobler task awaits thy hand;*
> *For what can war, but endless war still breed,*
> *Till truth, and right from violence be freed,*
> *And public faith cleared from the shameful brand*
> *Of public fraud.*

Milton did not want *Paradise Lost* to be about war, as he makes clear in Book IX: he wished his poem to have a 'higher argument' (IX. 27–9, 42). Since war is anyway an inconclusive means of settling differences on the side of 'truth and right', the different kinds of warfare, down to the most technologically advanced weapons such as cannon, used in the War in Heaven, might be intended to highlight its pointlessness, particularly for angels. An alternative view, however, has been put forward by C. S. Lewis, who claims that, since Milton's understanding of the nature of angels was Platonic, in that he believed them to be corporeal, a war such as he describes is perfectly reasonable. He writes:

> There is nothing unreasonable in giving the angels armour; though their airy bodies cannot be killed (i.e. reduced to inorganic matter) because they re-unite after cleavage with such 'admirable celerity', they can be damaged and hurt. A casing of some suitable inorganic material would therefore be a real protection. It is also reasonable that this armour, when opposed to the unfamiliar attack of artillery, should prove a hindrance rather than a help, by reducing the nimbleness of contraction, dilation and locomotion which the aereal body would have had when unencumbered.[7]

What as readers we can do, while keeping these issues in mind, is share in the vividness of the experience of war as Milton describes it. The Russian film director and theorist, Sergei Eisenstein, in his book *The Film Sense* (1943), selected three passages from Book VI of *Paradise Lost* which he arranged as 'shooting-scripts', because, he wrote,

> *Paradise Lost* itself is a first-rate school in which to study montage and audio-visual relationships ... Milton is particularly fine in battle scenes. Here his personal experience and eye-witness observations are frequently embodied ... Studying the pages of his poem ... we become extraordinarily enriched in experience of the audio-visual distribution of images.[8]

God's assembled troops march in perfect formation, while 'far in the horizon to the north' Satan's troops hurry forward, hoping for a surprise victory (VI. 79, 85). (It is of interest that, in the sonnet to Fairfax cited above, Milton refers to how 'the false North displays/Her broken league'.

This is a reference to the change of allegiance by the Scots from the Parliamentarian to the Royalist side – they were defeated by Cromwell at Preston in the month the sonnet was written. By this analogy, God becomes momentarily identified with Cromwell and Satan with Charles I a few months before his execution.) When the battle lines are drawn Abdiel steps forward, calls Satan a fool for opposing the omnipotent, and, referring to his own solitary opposition to Satan in the war council, says 'now learn too late/How few sometimes may know, when thousands err' (VI. 147–8). Satan scornfully asserts, in accordance with the agreement of the war council, that he will 'allow/Omnipotence to none', and taunts his opponents with servility rather than a love of freedom (VI. 158–9, 169). Abdiel now makes his famous identification of freedom with serving God (discussed above, in the previous section): 'God and nature bid the same,/... This is servitude,/To serve the unwise .../Thy self not free, but to thyself enthralled' (VI. 176–81). He then strikes the first blow, a massive strike on Satan's head, which causes him to recoil ten paces.

The war begins:

Now storming fury rose,
And clamour such as heard in heaven till now
Was never, arms on armour clashing brayed
Horrible discord, and the madding wheels
Of brazen chariots raged; dire was the noise
Of conflict; over head the dismal hiss
Of fiery darts in flaming volleys flew,
And flying vaulted either host with fire.

(VI. 207–14)

Satan displays 'prodigious power', but does not meet his equal in arms until he sees Michael felling 'squadrons at once' with his huge sword, held in two hands (VI. 247, 251). Michael, hoping to end the war there and then, addresses Satan: go to hell, he says, and take your misery, malice, and violence with you. No windy threats from you, says Satan, we mean to win, 'or turn this heaven it self into the hell/Thou fablest, here however to dwell free,/If not to reign' (VI. 291–3). Now follows a stupendous chivalric single combat between Satan and Michael, 'fit to decide the empire of great heaven' (VI. 303). Michael's sword proves the stronger, however, and cuts Satan's sword in half, as well as cutting off all Satan's right side (VI. 325–7). It was then that 'Satan first knew pain' – at least as far as our narrator Raphael knows: Sin has earlier in the poem reminded Satan that he first knew pain at the war council (VI. 327; II. 752–3). Being an angel, Satan's 'ethereal substance' soon heals up, though his armour is now stained with his angelic blood, or 'nectarous humour', and he is left 'gnashing for anguish and despite [i.e. 'spite'] and shame/To find himself not matchless' (VI. 332–4, 340–41). Meanwhile, other single combats take place, though Raphael is reluctant to name all the defeated devils, since it might 'eternize' their names on earth (VI. 374). At the end of the first day's fighting the rebels flee ignominiously. The loyalists feel no pain, being 'impenetrably armed', but the rebels, as a result of their disobedience, feel fear and pain for the first time.

At their strategic talks that night, Satan raises morale by commending his followers for their military achievements. They have proved two things, he says: one is that God cannot be omnipotent, otherwise they would have been totally defeated by the end of the first day – 'And if one day, why not eternal days?'; and the other is that, despite the new experience of pain, they are 'incapable of mortal injury' (VI. 424, 434). Of course, Satan is mistaken about the former issue, though, as we have seen, that is part of a major literary as well as theological problem deeply embedded in the text. Satan anyway recommends better weapons for the next day's battle. Nisroc, one of his leaders, complains about the effects of pain when fighting against those who don't feel it, and demands a new invention – the first escalation in armaments as a result of new technology. What Satan produces is gunpowder and cannon:

> *These in their dark nativity the deep*
> *Shall yield us pregnant with infernal flame,*
> *Which into hollow engines long and round*
> *Thick-rammed, at the other bore with touch of fire*
> *Dilated and infuriate shall send forth*
> *From far with thundering noise among our foes*
> *Such implements of mischief as shall dash*
> *To pieces, and o'erwhelm whatever stands*
> *Adverse.*
>
> (VI. 482–90)

They work all night to produce a secret Mark I version.

Day Two of the war begins with Zophiel, the loyalists' lookout, warning of the slow and orderly advance of the rebels. He conjectures that they should expect a 'rattling storm of arrows barbed with fire' (VI. 546). Satan, in a punning speech, commands his troops to divide and reveal the new weapon. Pretending to seek a truce, he commands his troops to stand ready 'if they like/Our overture [i.e. 'opening', both of pretended negotiations, and of the cannons' mouths]', while 'we discharge [i.e. 'fulfil' and 'shoot'] Freely our part', and 'briefly touch [i.e. 'refer to' and 'ignite']/What we propound, and loud that all may hear' (VI. 562–7). Revealed are three hollowed tree-trunks in a row. The powder is ignited, and the effect is described by Raphael with the imagery of vomit and faeces:

> *Immediate in a flame,*
> *But soon obscured with smoke, all heaven appeared,*
> *From those deep* ***throated*** *engines* ***belched****, whose roar*
> ***Embowelled*** *with outrageous noise the air,*
> *And all her* ***entrails*** *tore,* ***disgorging*** *foul*
> *Their devilish* ***glut****, chained thunderbolts and hail*
> *Of iron globes, which on the victor host*
> *Levelled, with such impetuous fury smote,*
> *That whom they hit, none on their feet might stand,*
> *Though standing else as rocks, but down they fell*
> *By thousands, angel on archangel rolled.*
>
> (VI. 584–94)

Observing the effect, Satan is in high spirits. The loyalists have been forced to scatter, or, as Satan with mocking irony puts it:

> *As they would dance, yet for a dance they seemed*
> *Somewhat extravagant and wild, perhaps*
> *For joy of offered peace: but I suppose*
> *If our proposals once again were heard*
> *We should compel them to a quick result.*
>
> (VI. 615–19)

Belial, enjoying the wit, joins in with an equally sophisticated pun, as he reflects that

> *... the terms we sent were terms of weight,*
> *Of hard contents, and full of force urged home,*
> *Such as we might perceive amused them all,*
> *And stumbled many.*
>
> (VI. 621–4)

However, their scoffing does not last long. The enraged loyalists throw heavenly hills (heaven being the original of everything on earth) on top of the rebels and their cannon. An image of total disorder follows that would have engulfed heaven had not the Father intervened.

The Father, having foreseen and permitted all this, assigns the Son, in a speech of embarrassing awkwardness for the reader, since the Son knows everything anyway, to end the otherwise endless war and gain the glory for so doing. The victory on the third day, as we later learn, is to become a foreshadowing of Christ's resurrection on the third day, signalling his victory over death.

Dawn on the third day of the war sees the Son ascending the throne of sapphire inlaid with amber, on the triumphal chariot of God – a symbol of his assumption of sovereignty. This is the first stage in the fulfilment of God's will, which will entail the Son's resignation 'when in the end/Thou shalt be all in all, and I in thee/For ever, and in me all whom thou lovest' – the fulfilment and end of history (VI. 731–3). Twenty thousand chariots follow him, and at his command the hills return to their places. Despite this, the rebels do not surrender, 'hope conceiving from despair', but prepare to fight (VI. 787). The Son addresses the loyalists to say that they need do nothing more: 'against me is all their rage .../Therefore to me their doom he hath assigned' (VI. 813, 817). He observes of them that 'by strength/They measure all, of other excellence/Not emulous, nor care they who excels' (VI. 820–22). The wrath of the Messiah is terrifying. All rebel resistance fails, and his chariot rides over their ruin. They become 'exhausted, spiritless, afflicted, fallen', before finally they are expelled from heaven (VI. 852). The Messiah drives them like a herd of goats

> *... before him thunderstruck, pursued*
> *With terrors and with furies to the bounds*
> *And crystal wall of heaven, which opening wide,*
> *Rolled inward, and a spacious gap disclosed*
> *Into the wasteful deep; the monstrous sight*
> *Strook them with horror backward, but far worse*
> *Urged them behind; headlong themselves they threw*
> *Down from the verge of heaven, eternal wrath*
> *Burnt after them to the bottomless pit.*
>
> (VI. 858–66)

They fall for nine days, until hell closes on them. (It was after they had been in hell for nine more days that the narrative in Book I opened.) The Messiah, meanwhile, returns to general acclamation, to sit 'at the right hand of bliss' (VI. 892).

Raphael does not fail to draw the moral of this story for Adam's benefit:

> *... let it profit thee to have heard*
> *By terrible example the reward*
> *Of disobedience; firm they might have stood,*
> *Yet fell; remember, and fear to transgress.*
>
> (VI. 909–12)

5 The Question of Knowledge: VII. 1–130

Milton is now half-way through his epic, and Raphael half-way through his narration (VII. 21). Milton interrupts the poem at this point for a very personal intervention, in the form of an address to his muse Urania, though, anxious to transcend pagan mythology, he asserts that it is 'the meaning, not the name I call' (VII. 5). Urania's presence with the Father at creation seems to imply that she may be identified with the Logos, or Son of God. If Aubrey is right that Milton began *Paradise Lost* 'about 2 yeares before the King came in, and finished about three yeares after the King's restauracion', it is a plausible conjecture that his sense of isolation as he stood firm in his anti-royalist principles before and after 1660 is reflected in his presentation of Abdiel's heroic stand against Satan and the rebels in Book V: 'Among the faithless, faithful only he' (V. 897).[9] Although after 1660 supporters of the Commonwealth were bitterly persecuted and sometimes executed, Milton did not change his antagonistic attitude towards the English monarchy, and he did not flee the country or even leave London. The new parliament ordered his arrest in June 1660, and in November he was imprisoned for about a month, being released on 15 December 1660. As Latin Secretary to Cromwell (virtually what we would consider Foreign Secretary), he might well have been hanged. Why he was not is not certain: perhaps Charles II was too clever a politician to put Milton in the dock, or perhaps Milton's brother Christopher, who had qualified as a barrister in that November, worked on his behalf behind the scenes. Or was it 'eternal providence'? Whatever the reasons, Milton's sense of prophetic solitariness in a hostile world is amplified at this point in the poem:

> *More safe I sing with mortal voice, unchanged*
> *To hoarse or mute, though fallen on evil days,*
> *On evil days though fallen, and evil tongues;*
> *In darkness, and with dangers compassed round,*
> *And solitude; yet not alone, while thou*
> *Visit'st my slumbers nightly, or when morn*
> *Purples the east: still govern thou my song,*
> *Urania, and fit audience find, though few.*
> *But drive far off the barbarous dissonance*
> *Of Bacchus and his revellers . . .*
>
> (VII. 24–33)

The search for a 'fit audience . . . though few' is an assertion of Abdiel-like integrity as Milton sings 'unchanged' amid the 'barbarous dissonance' of Restoration London.

So Milton begins the most joyful book of his poem with Adam's 'desire to know' about his origins and about the creation of heaven and earth (VII. 61). The question of knowledge, as we have seen, is ultimately a question of power, and is crucial to Satan's temptation, which results in the Fall. Here also it is the central issue. Milton makes Adam almost over-emphasize the point that the knowledge he is asking for is not a threat to the divine order. Adam expresses gratitude for what Raphael has already told him, 'which human knowledge could not reach', and promises to 'observe/Immutably his sovereign will' (VII. 75–9). So also, in asking for more information about the creation of the earth, Adam makes it clear that his purpose is not to 'explore secrets', which would be threatening to the established order, but 'the more/To magnify his works, the more we know' (VII. 95–7). Raphael agrees to reveal 'knowledge within bounds', such as will best serve 'to glorify the maker' (VII. 116, 120), and in one simile combines the central themes and images of the poem – knowledge, food, and self-restraint:

> *But knowledge is as food, and needs no less*
> *Her temperance over appetite, to know*
> *In measure what the mind may well contain,*
> *Oppresses else with surfeit, and soon turns*
> *Wisdom to folly, as nourishment to wind.*
>
> (VII. 126–30)

6 Raphael's Account of the Creation of the Universe: VII. 131–640

Raphael takes up again the story which he left off in Book VI with the Son's casting of Satan, now identified as Lucifer, and his followers into hell. God now makes explicit the plan of which rumours have already spread (see I. 651–4; II. 345–51, 830–35; III, 678–80; X. 481–2). This plan is to create 'another world' inhabited by creatures who will replace the fallen angels, and thus subvert Satan's pride in the harm he has done by seducing so many angels to his cause (VII. 155). Since 'rumours' of such a plan might imply that God was taken by surprise by Satan's rebellion or the extent of its success, or that therefore God was not free to act without compulsion, we may agree to accept that the rumours concerned only the *timing* of the plan and not the plan itself. The plan also entails that the inhabitants of this new world will be tested for obedience and eventually graduate to heaven: 'And earth be changed to heaven, and heaven to earth,/One kingdom, joy and union without end' (VII. 160–61). The creation would be done by the Son – 'speak thou, and be it done' – and in this metaphysical sense the Son is the Logos, or Word, or agent, of God.

The Son setting out on his creative mission to Chaos is a heavenly anticipation of Satan's departure on his destructive mission from hell through Chaos, already described in Book II. The gates of heaven open like this, for instance:

> *... heaven opened wide*
> *Her ever during gates, harmonious sound*
> *On golden hinges moving, to let forth*
> *The king of glory in his powerful Word*
> *And Spirit coming to create new worlds.*
>
> (VII. 205–9)

– whereas the gates of hell opened (or, are to open, since it is yet future) in this way:

> *... on a sudden open fly*
> *With impetuous recoil and jarring sound*
> *The infernal doors, and on their hinges grate*
> *Harsh thunder, that the lowest bottom shook*
> *Of Erebus.*
>
> (II. 879–83)

The Son calms the discord of Chaos, and, with 'golden compasses', circumscribes the bounds of creation (VII. 225). This is not creation from nothing, since God 'fills/Infinitude', but it is a matter of giving form and order to the Chaos from which God had previously chosen to withdraw himself (VII. 168–71).

From this point onwards Book VII is a paraphrase and expansion of the description of the six days of creation in the first chapter of Genesis. Hardly a phrase from the Authorised Version of 1611 is omitted, but the strength of Milton's elaboration of the biblical account lies in the sense of movement and of harmoniousness which he introduces. On the first day light is created, and, though the sun is not created until the fourth day, Milton avoids the old theological debate caused by this apparent inconsistency by simply stating that the light was as yet 'in a cloudy tabernacle' (VII. 248).

On the second day the 'firmament', or atmosphere, is created which fills the 'world', or universe. On the outside of the universe, surrounding the firmament, is the 'firm opacous [i.e. 'opaque'] globe' on which Satan lands after his journey from hell (III. 75, 418). On the third day dry land appears, as the water which until then had covered the embryo earth withdraws to reveal mountains. This results in deep oceans, corresponding in size to the mountains, and also rivers, as the water runs down to the seas and oceans. All is in proportion, designed by the golden compasses. Though there was considerable theological opinion that mountains did not appear until after Noah's flood – on the basis that the first mountains mentioned in the Bible are the 'mountains of Ararat', on which the ark comes to rest – Milton here takes the view that mountains were part of the original creation (Genesis 8:4). Paradise itself, we remember, is set on a mountain (IV. 226). Also on the third day vegetation appears. Milton's description emphasizes the dance-like activity and harmony, and also fruitfulness, of the emergence of the first living things on earth:

> *. . . the bare earth, till then*
> *Desert and bare, unsightly, unadorned,*
> *Brought forth the tender grass whose verdure clad*
> *Her universal face with pleasant green,*
> *Then herbs of every leaf, that sudden flowered*
> *Opening their various colours, and made gay*
> *Her bosom smelling sweet: and these scarce blown*
> *Forth flourished thick the clustering vine, forth crept*
> *The swelling gourd, up stood the corny reed*
> *Embattled in her field: and the humble shrub,*
> *And bush with frizzled hair implicit: last*
> *Rose as in dance the stately trees, and spread*
> *Their branches hung with copious fruit; or gemmed*
> *Their blossoms: with high woods the hills were crowned,*
> *With tufts the valleys and each fountain side,*
> *With borders long the rivers. That earth now*
> *Seemed like to heaven, a seat where gods might dwell.*
> (VII. 313–29)

On the fourth day the sun, moon and stars (including the planets) were created. The light created on the first day is placed 'in the sun's orb, made porous to receive/And drink the liquid light' (VII. 361–2). Taking up the metaphor of light as a fluid, the stars are described as drawing light from the sun in their 'golden urns' (VII. 365). The moon is the sun's 'mirror, with full face borrowing her light/From him, for other light she needed none' (VII. 377–8). That the moon shone with reflected light had been an observation of Galileo's, and the gender associations here, of a male sun and a female moon, we may notice, reinforce the assumed subservient status of the female.

The fifth day sees the creation of sea creatures and birds, who reproduce with amazing fecundity and variety. Shoals of fish, seals and dolphins, leviathans, eagles and storks, cranes, smaller birds, swans, cocks – earth teems with life, and all is in motion:

> *From branch to branch the smaller birds with song*
> *Solaced the woods, and spread their painted wings*
> *Till even, nor then the solemn nightingale*
> *Ceased warbling, but all night tuned her soft lays:*
> *Others on silver lakes and rivers bathed*
> *Their downy breast; the swan with arched neck*
> *Between her white wings mantling proudly, rows*
> *Her state with oary feet: yet oft they quit*
> *The dank, and rising on stiff pennons, tower*
> *The mid aerial sky: others on ground*
> *Walked firm; the crested cock whose clarion sounds*
> *The silent hours, and the other* [i.e. the peacock] *whose gay train*
> *Adorns him, coloured with the florid hue*
> *Of rainbows and starry eyes.*
>
> (VII. 433–46)

On the sixth day appear the beasts of the earth, both wild and domesticated. The cattle appear 'in broad herds upsprung', whereas the tawny lion half appears, 'pawing to get free/His hinder parts, then springs as broke from bonds,/And rampant shakes his brinded [i.e. 'brownish'] mane' (VII. 464–6). Tiger, stag, elephant ('behemoth'), hippopotamus, and crocodile all appear, as do creatures which after the Fall are to become pests – insects, small crawling creatures ('worm'), and the serpent. The ant ('emmet') and the bee also appear, examples of the virtues of 'commonalty', or democracy, and industriousness. Though earth now 'in her rich attire/Consummate lovely smiled', something yet remained: the 'master work', which was to be a creature endowed with reason who would govern the rest of creation in devotion to God (VII. 501–14). So Adam is created from the dust of the ground, and becomes a living soul. With a female consort, he is commanded to 'be fruitful, multiply, and fill the earth', and is given dominion over all living things on earth. He is then brought to Paradise, with the warning not to eat of the tree 'which tasted works knowledge of good and evil' (VII. 543). At this the creator retires from his work, 'desisting, though unwearied', and returns with triumphal acclamation to the Father in heaven: mission accomplished.

The seventh day is declared a day of rest, and is celebrated with joyful music and song in recognition of the creation:

Great are thy works, Jehovah, infinite
Thy power; what thought can measure thee or tongue
Relate thee; greater now in thy return
Than from the giant angels; thee that day
Thy thunders magnified; but to create
Is greater than created to destroy.
. . . Thrice happy men,
And sons of men, whom God hath thus advanced,
Created in his image, there to dwell
And worship him, and in reward to rule
Over his works, on earth, in sea, or air,
And multiply a race of worshippers
Holy and just: thrice happy if they know
Their happiness, and persevere upright.

(VII. 602–32)

7 The Nature and Purpose of the Universe: VIII. 1–202

The joyful story of the creation leaves Adam stunned. His thirst for knowledge is largely allayed, but not quite. Something 'of doubt' remains, and this doubt is symptomatic of Milton's own conflict between the Christian and what we might call the 'humanist' view of the universe. It is a conflict which ultimately he cannot resolve, and which therefore raises again the whole issue of the benefits or otherwise of knowledge.

The old certainties of the Ptolemaic universe were comforting to the Christian: the earth at the centre of the finite universe implied mankind at the centre of the creator's thoughts and purposes. Seventeenth-century telescopes, however, had raised queries not only about whether the earth was in fact central, but also about whether the apparently vast infinitudes of space were entirely created for the benefit and enjoyment of humans, or whether there were possibly other inhabited worlds in space. Speculation on these issues was rife, and Milton, in his role as the inspired poet, addresses them here also. This is the 'doubt' that Adam feels: the earth is so small compared with the 'spaces incomprehensible' of the stars that, if the function of the heavens is merely to shine for the benefit of earth, how is it that 'nature wise and frugal could commit/Such disproportions' (VIII. 20, 26–7)? We remember that this is basically the question that

Eve had asked Adam the previous day: 'But wherefore all night long shine these, for whom/This glorious sight, when sleep hath shut all eyes?' (IV. 657–8). Then Adam had answered that the function of the stars was to ensure that the original 'total darkness' before creation did not return, and that anyway spiritual creatures observe the heavens at all times and praise God's works when humans are asleep.

Adam's present question to Raphael leads to Eve's withdrawal from the conversation to visit the garden, perhaps because she has heard a satisfactory answer already from Adam. Certainly, as Milton makes clear, she does not leave because she is bored or out of her depth:

> *Yet went she not, as not with such discourse*
> *Delighted, or not capable her ear*
> *Of what was high: such pleasure she reserved,*
> *Adam relating, she sole auditress;*
> *Her husband the relater she preferred*
> *Before the angel, and of him to ask*
> *Chose rather; he, she knew would intermix*
> *Grateful digressions, and solve high dispute*
> *With conjugal caresses, from his lip*
> *Not words alone pleased her. O when meet now*
> *Such pairs, in love and mutual honour joined?*
>
> (VIII. 48–58)

The concluding rhetorical question reflects Milton's own aspirations for an ideal marriage of mutuality, for which he argued cogently in his divorce tracts of 1643–5, though again the expressed desire for mutuality coexists with a portrayal of the woman as implicitly the passive partner – 'Adam relating, she sole auditress'. As Eve departs, these lines occur:

> *And from about her shot darts of desire*
> *Into all eyes to wish her still in sight.*
>
> (VIII. 62–3)

Christopher Ricks has persuasively argued that the momentary pause on 'desire' when it comes at the end of the line allows us to anticipate the carnal 'desire' which follows the Fall, before we realize that the desire here is totally innocent, and in fact the desire of others to be in sight of her 'winning graces' (IX. 1013; VIII. 61). As he comments, 'The potential danger, then, is expressed in the potential syntax'.[10] The subtlety is ruined if the word-order is transposed: 'And from about her shot into all eyes/Darts of desire to wish her still in sight'.

Raphael now, in the absence of Eve, addresses himself to Adam's 'doubt'. Basically he cannot answer Adam's question, though he produces various astronomical hypotheses, and in the end he retreats behind the position that the 'great architect' wisely concealed from man and angel certain facts about the universe such as 'whether heaven move or earth' (VIII. 70). He proposes that we ought to admire rather than investigate the universe – the old-fashioned Christian view – and suggests that the struggle to understand only makes God laugh at men's 'quaint opinions' (VIII. 78). But then, in contradiction of the implications of this argument, Raphael goes on to provide 'quaint opinions' himself. First, against the argument that greater, brighter bodies should not serve smaller, duller ones, such as earth, it is wrong to assume that size and brightness equate with excellence: the earth, though not bright, may contain more good, in Adam, than the sun. Then, the vast reaches of space may be there to remind man of his minor place: 'that man may know he dwells not in his own' (VIII. 103). Further, the inexpressible speeds and distances involved in an earth-centred universe show God's omnipotence. But, on the other hand, heaven is so far from earth that man's view may be in error. 'What if the sun/Be centre to the world', Raphael asks, without committing himself (VIII. 122–3). Adam's idea of a central 'sedentary earth' might after all be an 'earth industrious' which fetches day by travelling east (VIII. 32, 137–8). And perhaps, since the sun shines on it too, the moon is designed for habitation, and perhaps other suns shine on other moons which are also inhabited? It is therefore not necessarily the case that the whole universe is intended to be 'desert and desolate' merely in order to provide a 'glimpse of light' for earth (VIII. 154–6).

These speculations, in the humanist tradition of inquiry, are, however, terminated by Raphael with an image that makes its point by containing the astronomical issue within an unquestioned gender stereotype, of dominant male sun and inoffensively gentle female earth:

> *But whether thus these things, or whether not,*
> *Whether the sun predominant in heaven*
> *Rise on the earth, or earth rise on the sun,*
> *He from the east his flaming road begin,*
> *Or she from west her silent course advance*
> *With inoffensive pace that spinning sleeps*
> *On her soft axle, while she paces even,*
> *And bears thee soft with the smooth air along,*
> *Solicit not thy thoughts with matters hid,*
> *Leave them to God above, him serve and fear.*
>
> (VIII. 159–68)

On being advised not to 'dream of other worlds', speculation which, ironically, Raphael himself has stimulated, Adam is apparently 'cleared of doubt' (VIII. 179). Thus Milton's conflict between Christian and humanist views is at the *explicit* level won by the Christian injunction not to probe into God's secrets: 'be lowly wise' (VIII. 173). *Implicitly*, however, since the resolution of the issues is not rationally satisfactory, this older Christian view is undermined. Adam's words, 'How fully hast thou satisfied me, pure/Intelligence of heaven', sound to us rather hollow.

There is, nevertheless, a consistent point here which Milton is arguing, which is echoed more than a century later in Wordsworth's poem, *The Prelude*, which takes up in a secular way some of the themes of *Paradise Lost* as well as its form. Wordsworth in the 1790s had a nervous breakdown, and described it in part like this:

> *Thus I fared . . . now believing,*
> *Now disbelieving, endlessly perplexed*
> *With impulse, motive, right and wrong, the ground*
> *Of moral obligation – what the rule,*
> *And what the sanction – till, demanding proof,*
> *And seeking it in every thing, I lost*
> *All feeling of conviction, and, in fine* [i.e. 'in the end'],
> *Sick, wearied out with contrarieties,*
> *Yielded up moral questions in despair.*[11]

Wordsworth had been bewildered by the big issues of political and philosophical allegiance in the revolutionary 1790s, and his 'cure' had come about by discovering a private 'self' in the non-contentious context of nature. Milton offers a warning, based on his questioning of his own political and philosophical allegiances in the 1650s, which implies a similar solution. Adam thanks Raphael for teaching him to live a private, or 'daily life':

> *. . . nor with perplexing thoughts*
> *To interrupt the sweet of life, from which*
> *God hath bid dwell far off all anxious cares,*
> *And not molest us, unless we our selves*
> *Seek them with wandering thoughts, and notions vain.*
> *But apt the mind or fancy is to rove*
> *Unchecked, and of her roving is no end;*
> *Till warned, or by experience taught, she learn,*
> *That not to know at large of things remote*
> *From use, obscure and subtle, but to know*

> *That which before us lies in daily life,*
> *Is the prime wisdom.*
>
> (VIII. 183–94)

Both Milton and Wordsworth came to find virtue in solitariness and withdrawal from political engagement.

8 Adam's Account of His and Eve's Creation: VIII. 203–653

Adam by now has listened to Raphael's talk for a long time – nearly three whole books of the poem. In line with the argument for the priority of 'daily life' over knowledge 'at large of things remote', Adam now offers to tell Raphael of his own creation as he remembers it, meanwhile courteously acknowledging, with another metaphor relating to taste, that Raphael's words 'bring to their sweetness no satiety' (VIII. 191, 193, 216). Raphael was away on the day of Adam's creation on a mission to check the security of the gates of hell, and here we see further Milton's problems in narrating omnipotence. Raphael was sent

> *To see that none thence issued forth a spy,*
> *Or enemy, while God was in his work,*
> *Lest he incensed at such eruption bold,*
> *Destruction with creation might have mixed.*
> *Not that they durst without his leave attempt,*
> *But us he sends upon his high behests*
> *For state, as sovereign king, and to inure* [i.e. 'habituate us to']
> *Our prompt obedience.*
>
> (VIII. 233–40)

Aside from the fear of upsetting the temperamental Father, here we see Raphael acknowledging that no one could escape hell without the Father's permission anyway ('Not that they durst without his leave attempt'), and then, as if realizing that therefore his mission had no purpose, justifying it as a ploy of the Father's to 'inure' obedience. This apparent afterthought serves only to highlight the insuperable narrative problem.

Adam proceeds to describe his creation in what becomes a gloss on Genesis 2, just as Book VII had been a gloss on Genesis 1. Adam's first memory is of being 'new waked from soundest sleep' (VIII. 253). He leaps to his feet and stands upright 'by quick instinctive motion', and as he observes the natural beauty around him his heart overflows with joy. He is able instantly to speak, and can name whatever he sees. He immediately asks around for information about his origins, feeling that he cannot be autonomous:

> *Tell, if ye saw, how came I thus, how here?*
> *Not of my self; by some great maker then,*
> *In goodness and in power pre-eminent;*
> *Tell me, how may I know him, how adore,*
> *From whom I have that thus I move and live,*
> *And feel that I am happier than I know.*
>
> (VIII. 277–82)

We are reminded of the song of the angels after the creation – 'thrice happy if they know/Their happiness' (VII. 631–2) – and also of the poignant lines at the end of the address to wedded love – 'O yet happiest if ye seek/No happier state, and know to know no more' (IV. 774–5). But we also remember the enticement of the temptation, both in Eve's dream – 'happy though thou are,/Happier thou mayst be' (V. 75–6) – and just prior to the Fall itself, in the promise of 'what might lead/To happier life, knowledge of good and evil' (IX. 696–7). Thus Adam's present 'happier than I know', in its dramatic irony, touches the question of the ephemerality of innocent happiness, and, by implication, the central doctrine of the Fortunate Fall. God appears to Adam as in a dream, and guides him to Paradise. Here God identifies himself as the creator, and gives Adam the command to look after the garden, followed by the 'rigid interdiction' not to eat of the tree 'whose operation brings/Knowledge of good and ill' on pain of death (VIII. 323–4, 334). Adam is made lord of all creation, and names the animals as they pass before him, naming implying that he understood their nature.

Despite this plethora of delight and authority, Adam is not completely happy, and, in expressing his sense of lack to God, he is subject to some teasing by him. This episode is the closest God comes to having a sense of humour and a personality that is not authoritarian. Perhaps this is because God here is really the Son, as agent of creation, or because the conversation is reported by Adam: in any case it is impossible to identify this genial figure on earth with the stern omnipotence we see in heaven (III. 384–91; VII. 163–4, 174–5; and Colossians 1:16; Hebrews 1:2). Adam wants a human companion, and expresses to God his need for what Milton saw as the prime function of marriage to fill:

> *. . . of fellowship I speak*
> *Such as I seek, fit to participate*
> *All rational delight.*
>
> (VIII. 389–91)

God answers, in effect, what about me? –

> *Seem I to thee sufficiently possessed*
> *Of happiness, or not? Who am alone*
> *From all eternity, for none I know*
> *Second to me or like, equal much less.*
>
> (VIII. 404–7)

To which Adam replies, yes, but you are already infinite, and do not need social communication, and anyway if you did you could deify any creature you wanted (VIII. 420, 429). I, on the other hand, have no one to communicate with on my own level. At which God owns up to his teasing: 'I, ere thou spakest,/Knew it not good for man to be alone', he says, and promises to bring 'thy likeness, thy fit help, thy other self' as a companion for Adam (VIII. 444–5, 450). Adam then falls asleep, and dreams of a bloody operation followed by a miraculous healing, in which a rib from his left side is removed and fashioned into a beautiful creature. Her looks, he says,

> *. . . from that time infused*
> *Sweetness into my heart, unfelt before,*
> *And into all things from her air inspired*
> *The spirit of love and amorous delight.*
>
> (VIII. 474–7)

Adam wakes to fear he has lost her, but, finding her, names her 'woman', and defines the principle of true marriage for his descendants: 'they shall be one flesh, one heart, one soul' (VIII. 499).

There is some evidence that, in the seventeenth century, female coyness or sexual refusal was more sexually exciting for men than it is commonly thought to be today. Numerous lyrics, from Donne to Marvell, celebrate this quality, and Milton has already mentioned Eve's 'sweet reluctant amorous delay' as an attractive feature of her love-making (IV. 311). This, however, poses a problem for the poet of Paradise. 'Virgin modesty' is a quality which arises from *social* behaviour, and it is hard to understand how it can have meaning otherwise (VIII. 501). When Adam leads Eve, who is 'blushing like the morn', to the nuptial bower, it is hard to understand why a person with no sexual experience, let alone shame or guilt, should blush (VIII. 511). Adam obviously feels pleasure at her blushing, and perhaps this derives from some sense of sexual authority. In any case, though Eve would 'not unsought be won', she is 'pure of sinful thought' (VIII. 503, 506). All of earth celebrates their union.

Adam now reveals to Raphael the strength of his passion for Eve, which we can see as ominous in view of the imminent Fall. His 'vehement desire' for her is different from his delight in the rest of creation (VIII. 526). He describes it thus:

> *... here passion first I felt,*
> *Commotion strange, in all enjoyments else*
> *Superior and unmoved, here only weak*
> *Against the charm of beauty's powerful glance.*
>
> (VIII. 530–33)

In these and the next twenty-six lines we can see the contradiction which underlies Adam's, and Milton's, attitude to woman, and the problems which come from attempting to rationalize and thus repress it. If Eve is wonderful enough to excite a perfect man's passionate love, how can she also be inferior to the man? Adam first blames himself, in the quoted lines, for being 'weak' in falling for her charms, but then blames 'nature' (really, of course, God) for not making him resistant ('proof enough'), for perhaps taking too much out along with the rib, and for making Eve too outwardly attractive – 'in outward show/Elaborate, of inward less exact' (VIII. 535, 538, 539). So Eve is inwardly inferior and outwardly less like God because less dominant, but still Adam finds her irresistibly attractive. The only solution is to rationalize this very attraction of mutual love into a degrading and folly-inducing attribute:

> *... yet when I approach*
> *Her loveliness, so absolute she seems*
> *And in her self complete, so well to know*
> *Her own, that what she wills to do or say,*
> *Seems wisest, virtuousest, discreetest, best;*
> *All higher knowledge in her presence falls*
> *Degraded, wisdom in discourse with her*
> *Looses discountenanced, and like folly shows;*
> *Authority and reason on her wait,*
> *As one intended first, not after made*
> *Occasionally* [i.e. 'as a secondary matter']*; and to consummate all,*
> *Greatness of mind and nobleness their seat*
> *Build in her loveliest, and create an awe*
> *About her, as a guard angelic placed.*
>
> (VIII. 546–59)

Raphael solemnly instructs Adam not to blame 'nature', but to be confident in God's wisdom. Adam must distinguish between loving Eve and subjecting himself to her. Erotic passion, Raphael argues, is shared by the animals, which shows that it is nothing special. Adam should love whatever in Eve is 'attractive, human, rational', in the sound confines of puritan self-discipline:

> *What higher in her society thou find'st*
> *Attractive, human, rational, love still;*
> *In loving thou dost well, in passion not,*
> *Wherein true love consists not; love refines*
> *The thoughts, and heart enlarges, hath his seat*
> *In reason, and is judicious, is the scale*
> *By which to heavenly love thou mayst ascend,*
> *Not sunk in carnal pleasure, for which cause*
> *Among the beasts no mate for thee was found.*
> (VIII. 586–94)

This celebration of the rational over the passionate is the fundamental theme of *Paradise Lost*, but here, presented as the subordination of love to reason, prepares the way for the condemnation of Adam after the Fall for 'worth in women overtrusting' (IX. 1183). It imposes on Adam and Eve's mutuality the taint of 'carnal pleasure', which belies the sensitivity and strength of their expressions of feeling for each other, both here and in Books IV and IX. The conflict between male superiority and male–female mutuality is once again exposed, to the explicit detriment of the woman. In his arguments for divorce, which would free people to find a suitable partner if they were locked in an unsuitable marriage, Milton had written in 1643:

> First we know St *Paul* saith, *It is better to marry then to burn*. Mariage therfore was giv'n as a remedy of that trouble: but what might this burning mean? Certainly not the meer motion of carnall lust ... What is it then but that desire which God put into *Adam* in Paradise before he knew the sin of incontinence; that desire which God saw it was not good that man should be left alone to burn in; the desire and longing to put off an unkindly solitarines by uniting another body, but not without a fit soule to his in the cheerfull society of wedlock. Which if it were so needfull before the fall, when man was much more perfect in himselfe, how much more is it needfull now against all the sorrows and casualties of this life to have an intimate and speaking help, a ready and reviving associate in marriage.[12]

Uniting with a fit soul is clearly much more than the 'carnal pleasure' which Raphael senses, and admonishes, in Adam's words. Adam is, to his credit, only 'half abashed' by Raphael's talk, and gives a spirited defence of his relationship with Eve (VIII. 595). What matters most, he says, is not sex, but

> *Those thousand decencies that daily flow*
> *From all her words and actions mixed with love*
> *And sweet compliance, which declare unfeigned*
> *Union of mind, or in us both one soul;*
> *Harmony to behold in wedded pair*
> *More grateful than harmonious sound to the ear.*
> (VIII. 601–6)

These do not subject him to her, he asserts: describing his passion does not mean he is dominated by it. Adam then, presumably with the half of him that is not abashed, turns the question on Raphael: do angels have sex? Raphael, blushing 'with a smile that glowed/Celestial rosy red', answers yes (VIII. 618–19). This is what we would expect since we have already heard that the angels feel 'real hunger' and eat real food (V. 437). Angelic sex is of a superior kind, in that, unencumbered by flesh, they can mix through total interpenetration. Thus Milton implicitly argues for the essential innocence of sexuality, and for the central importance of *union* as its true function, rather than mere reproduction as among animals. (We later learn, in fact, that there are no female angels (X. 893; but see I. 423–31).)

By now it is nearing 6 p.m., or sunset, in Paradise, and Raphael takes his leave with a final warning to Adam not to let his passion sway his judgment: 'stand fast; to stand or fall/Free in thine own arbitrament it lies' (VIII. 641–2). Adam thanks him and asks him to 'oft return' (VIII. 651). (Raphael does not say goodbye to Eve.) In fact, he never does return to Adam and Eve: the next angelic presence is to be the stern archangel Michael, who expels the happy couple from Paradise (XII. 637–43).

V The Fourth Day: Paradise – One Week Later

1 'The better fortitude/Of patience'; IX. 1–47

The opening of Book IX signals that the climax of the story is imminent. The muse is not directly addressed in this fourth and last invocation, but the narrative voice begins for the only time with a negative, describing the end of close communion between man and 'God or angel guest', and continuing sadly, 'I now must change/Those notes to tragic' (IX. 1, 5, 6). The pastoral of Paradise is now to change genre to tragedy, all within the framework of the epic. The opening of the poem, with its conjunction of the idea of 'taste' and a world of woe, has already been echoed in Book VIII in God's command to Adam (VIII. 327–33). Here it is echoed with a significant shift:

> *... on the part of heaven*
> *Now alienated, distance and distaste,*
> *Anger and just rebuke, and judgment given,*
> *That brought into this world a world of woe.*
>
> (IX. 8–11)

The 'taste' of the human pair has here become the 'distaste' of heaven. The word 'taste' will occur twenty-five times in one form or another in Book IX, out of the sixty-five times it occurs in the whole poem.

But although the theme of man's Fall is tragic, it is actually, argues Milton, *more* heroic than the conventional heroism of epic and romance, such as Achilles' pursuit of Hector in the *Iliad*, or the deeds of legendary knights in fictional battles. This is because *Paradise Lost* essentially celebrates 'the better fortitude/Of patience and heroic martyrdom' which has hitherto remained 'unsung' (IX. 31–2). While a supporter of Cromwell in 1652, the year in which he became totally blind and in which his first wife and only son died, Milton had written a sonnet 'To the Lord General Cromwell' praising him as 'our chief of men', yet warning that 'peace hath her victories/No less renowned than war'. Now, ten years later, following the collapse of all his aspirations for the English people, and much personal tragedy, how much more was Milton aware, in the changed circumstances of a re-established monarchy, of the need for patience and heroic endurance. Battles seemed trivial compared with the immense individual struggle necessitated for all as a result of the story Milton was telling. His story has a 'higher argument' which can elevate the name of epic, and visitations from his nocturnal muse (Milton composed *Paradise Lost* mostly at night or in the early morning) will ensure that his enterprise succeeds (VII. 29; IX. 22, 42, 47).

2 Satan's Return to Paradise: IX. 48–191

After the long conversation between Adam and Raphael recorded in Books V to VIII a week has elapsed, and it is now midnight. It was at midnight that Satan had first arrived at the universe nine days earlier, and midnight on the next night that he had been expelled from Paradise by Gabriel, after being found 'squat like a toad' at the ear of Eve (III. 557; IV. 800, 1015). For more than a week Satan has been flying round the earth in permanent darkness by keeping in the earth's shadow (IX. 63, 67). Once more, despite the alerted cherubim on guard, Satan finds his way past them into Paradise. He immerses himself in the Tigris river, which flows underground and rises in a fountain by the tree of life, so that, symbolically, evil enters Paradise at the very source of life, with the waters of life. In a parody of Adam's understanding the nature of every creature when he named them, Satan, on his circuits of the earth, had 'considered every creature' for the purpose of finding the one who would provide the most appropriate disguise for his intentions (VIII. 352–3; IX. 84). He has selected the serpent, since the deviousness of the snake's nature would mean that no 'diabolic power' would be suspected within him (IX. 95).

Just as on his first arrival on earth on Niphates' summit, so here, on his second arrival directly in Paradise, Satan makes a passionate soliloquy, of about the same length. The former was his first, and this is his last; the former was addressed to the sun, and this to the earth; the former followed his metamorphosis into a cherub (when, at the end of Book III, he had enquired of Uriel the way to Paradise), and this is followed by his metamorphosis into a serpent. Thus is signalled Satan's decline: he is no longer the statesman and military leader of Books I and II, but a destructive consciousness, eaten up with envy and malice. His emotional soliloquy at this point, though caused, we are told, by 'inward grief', expresses no hint of pity, and does not consider the idea of repentance, as did his first soliloquies in Book IV (IV. 32–113, 358–92; IX. 97). It is tinged with regret – 'With what delight could I have walked thee round' – and expresses the same sense of isolation from the beauties of earth – 'the more I see/Pleasures about me, so much more I feel/Torment within me, as from the hateful siege/Of contraries' – but it is essentially positive in its malice (IX. 144, 119–22). Satan does not hope to be less miserable himself, but only to make others the same: 'For only in destroying I find ease/To my relentless thoughts' (IX. 129–30). He queries God's omniscience, in suggesting that earth was made 'with second thoughts' on his part, as an improvement on a not quite good enough earlier effort at creation, and he still expresses doubt as to whether God had created the angels or whether they were 'self-begot' (IX. 101, 146–7). At the time of the rebellion in heaven he had responded to the suggestion that he and the other angels were created, rather than autonomous, as 'strange point and new!', though in his first soliloquy he seemed already to have come to terms with it, and referred to himself as 'created' (V. 855, 60; IV. 43). Now just before his big test of nerve at the temptation he perhaps needs to bolster his courage by reopening the question. God is now for him only 'almighty styled', the question of omnipotence having been one of the subjects of debate in the council in Book II which had commissioned him to undertake his present errand (IX. 137). He now even attributes the creation of mankind to himself, thereby assuming his own inferior motive of revenge to be God's:

> *... I in one night freed*
> *From servitude inglorious well-nigh half*
> *The angelic name, and thinner left the throng*
> *Of his adorers: he to be avenged,*
> *And to repair his numbers thus impaired, ...*
> *Determined to advance into our room*
> *A creature formed of earth, and him endow,*
> *Exalted from so base original,*
> *With heavenly spoils, our spoils.*
>
> (IX. 140–51)

His hurt pride, malice, and vengeful spite are now his personal motives for finding a serpent in which, in a word which parodies Messiah's later sacrifice, to 'incarnate', and fire his revenge (IX. 166). Using the imagery of firearms ('recoils ... aimed ... fall short'), which remind us of his first approach to earth and of the War in Heaven, he sets up his attack on mankind in language that has lost the sense of 'public reason just' that had been the main part of his earlier motivation (IV. 17; VI. 482–90; IV. 389; II. 448):

> *... Revenge, at first though sweet,*
> *Bitter ere long back on it self recoils;*
> *Let it; I reck* [i.e. 'care'] *not, so it light well aimed,*
> *Since higher I fall short, on him who next*

Provokes my envy, this new favourite
Of heaven, this man of clay, son of despite,
Whom us the more to spite his maker raised
From dust: spite then with spite is best repaid.

(IX. 171–8)

After a 'midnight search', Satan, creeping through Paradise like a black mist, finds a suitable serpent 'in labyrinth of many a round self rolled' (IX. 181, 183). He enters the creature's mouth without even waking it up, and waits for morning, the fateful morning of the day of the Fall. Within thirty-six hours mankind will have lost Paradise.

3 The Separation of Adam and Eve: IX. 192–411

Eve has the first and last words in the fateful conversation which leads to her separation from Adam. Her first speech demonstrates, with subtle tragic irony, her self-will and desire for independence from Adam, as her language anticipates the Fall. This 'new' Eve is the consequence of Satan's effect on her when he was found 'squat like a toad' at her ear in Book IV, which led to the dream she recounted in Book V (IV. 800; V. 28–93). Eve complains that, until they have help, it is hard to keep up with their assigned task of subduing the earth, and the language she uses is resonant with significance:

. . . but till more hands
Aid us, the work under our labour grows,
Luxurious by restraint; what we by day
Lop overgrown, or prune, or prop, or bind,
One night or two with wanton growth derides
Tending to wild. Thou therefore now advise
Or hear what to my mind first thoughts present,
Let us divide our labours, thou where choice
Leads thee, or where most needs, whether to wind
The woodbine round this arbour, or direct
The clasping ivy where to climb, while I
In yonder spring of roses intermixed
With myrtle, find what to redress till noon.

(IX. 207–19)

The words 'luxurious . . . wanton . . . wild', though innocent here, carry anticipations of their fallen meanings – lecherous . . . unchaste . . . unrestrained.[1] Paradise is now 'tending to wild' with these words of Eve, in fact to the 'wild woods' which Adam perceives after his decision to die with Eve (IX. 910). The word 'restraint' also takes us back to the start of the poem, where it refers to God's prohibition on the eating of the fruit of the tree of knowledge, and equally forward to Eve's actual eating of the fruit, which she greedily engorges 'without restraint' (I. 32; IX. 791). Eve's self-will is shown in her apparent invitation to Adam to 'advise/Or hear' immediately followed by her 'first thoughts', forcing him to hear. The ivy around the elm had been used in Book V as a symbol of true love – 'she spoused about him twines/Her marriageable arms' – whereas the rose was frequently used as a symbol of human frailty (V. 216–17). Thus Eve's suggestion that Adam should look after the ivy while she does the roses is particularly rich with implications: she shortly ties up the 'drooping unsustained' roses though she herself is 'fairest unsupported flower' (IX. 430, 432). The tragic irony is in her suggestion that, if they worked together, they might be distracted into casual chat by some 'object new' (IX. 222). The new object in Paradise is, as we know, the diabolic serpent, and now above all the unsupported needs support.

Adam's reply is rich in further ironies. 'Nothing lovelier can be found/In woman, than to study household good,/And good works in her husband to promote' is his response to Eve's suggestion for dividing their labours: but no good, for household or husband, comes of it (IX. 232–4). The imagery of eating is central to *Paradise Lost*: the first two lines of the poem speak of 'fruit' and 'taste', Raphael comes to lunch in Book V and eats real food, and in Paradise supper has to be earned. But Adam points out that there are also other sorts of food:

> *Yet not so strictly hath our Lord imposed*
> *Labour, as to debar us when we need*
> *Refreshment, whether food, or talk between,*
> *Food of the mind, or this sweet intercourse*
> *Of looks and smiles, for smiles from reason flow,*
> *To brute denied, and are of love the food,*
> *Love not the lowest end of human life.*
>
> (IX. 235–41)

Talk 'feeds' the mind, and smiles deriving from reason 'feed' love, which is the purpose (or 'end'), and not the lowest, of life itself. Life is not just about efficient and successful gardening. Reason, smiles, love, talk, delight – this sustaining complex is about to be disrupted because Eve is apparently 'satiate' with too much conversation (IX. 248). Their malicious foe, Adam warns, is 'greedy' to find them separate, since their conjugal love excites his envy more than anything else (IX. 257, 263–4). He advises

Eve to stay by his side, to stay by her husband 'who guards her, or with her the worst endures' (IX. 269). Another dramatic irony, since he will choose to endure 'the worst' as a result of her *not* staying by his side.

Eve in response stands on her dignity: I really didn't think that you would think so badly of someone you love! But here emerges a problem for Milton as great as that we have already noticed of narrating omnipotence: that of narrating innocence. Just as omnipotence and omniscience destroy the credibility of a narrative, so does innocence. Eve cannot know about fraud, hypocrisy, or lying while innocent. How can we then blame her for the impending Fall? Surely she is only acting according to the dictates of her nature in believing all she is told? Again, how can she say the following to Adam, when she cannot know fraud or fear?

> *His* [i.e. 'the foe's'] *fraud is then thy fear, which plain infers*
> *Thy equal fear that my firm faith and love*
> *Can by his fraud be shaken or seduced;*
> *Thoughts, which how found they harbour in thy breast*
> *Adam, misthought of her to thee so dear?*
>
> (IX. 285–9)

This leads some to the conclusion that Eve's real fall took place when Satan sat at her ear in the shape of a toad, which led to her dream in which her appetite was quickened by the 'pleasant savoury smell' of the forbidden fruit held to her mouth (IV. 800; V. 83–4). But this suggestion merely displaces the narrative problem rather than solves it, because it is insoluble. Perfect innocence, like omnipotence and omniscience, is a dream which is unrealizable in narrative. It merely produces contradictions in the story which show up its own unreality. The narrative 'unmasks' the fact that constructing a lost 'innocence', like constructing omnipotence, has a design on us and is part of a system of attempted social control which tells us that a lost state of trouble-free existence is apparently retrievable through certain forms of obedience, or by fearing a vengeful almighty. Milton deals with this problem of presenting a story in which innocence is blamed for falling into sin with two strategies. One, the argument used by Adam when Eve told him of her dream in Book V, is to say that an innocent creature can dream of evil without blame when the faculty of reason is asleep, though this does not explain how she could *understand* it (V. 117–21). The other is to emphasize the weakness of the woman, who needs the man more than he needs her, in order to overcome her self-will and self-love – though this merely displaces the problem of innocence on to the man. There is finally no solution.

Adam now addresses Eve as 'daughter of God and man', in order to emphasize her dependence on him, out of whose body she was made (IX. 291). He assures her that she is entirely free from 'sin and blame', but argues that though she would, of course, resist temptation on her own, the very fact of it is an insult from which he wishes to protect her by their staying together, since that would reduce the likelihood of temptation, or at least deflect it to him. He feels more wise and watchful in her presence, where shame would prevent him from being overcome: why does not she feel the same way, he asks?

Eve's reply, with 'accent sweet', is her most interesting speech in terms of its implications for our understanding of the poem. She essentially says that virtue without the confidence that comes from testing it not only fails to produce happiness, but is also not really virtue:

> *If this be our condition, thus to dwell*
> *In narrow circuit straitened by a foe,*
> *Subtle or violent, we not endued*
> *Single with like defence, wherever met,*
> *How are we happy, still in fear of harm? . . .*
> *And what is faith, love, virtue unassayed*
> *Alone, without exterior help sustained?*
>
> (IX. 322–6, 335–6)

This is almost exactly the position adopted nearly twenty years earlier by Milton in his argument against censorship to the English Parliament:

> I cannot praise a fugitive and cloister'd vertue, unexercis'd and unbreath'd, that never sallies out and sees her adversary, but slinks out of the race, where that immortall garland is to be run for, nòt without dust and heat . . . That vertue therefore which is but a youngling in the contemplation of evill, and knows not the utmost that vice promises to her followers, and rejects it, is but a blank vertue, not a pure . . . Many there be that complain of divin Providence for suffering *Adam* to transgresse, foolish tongues! when God gave him reason, he gave him freedom to choose, for reason is but choosing; he had bin else a meer artificiall *Adam*, such an *Adam* as he is in the motions [i.e. 'puppet shows': cf. 'movies']. We our selves esteem not of that obedience, or love, or gift, which is of force: God therefore left him free, set before him a provoking object, ever almost in his eyes; herein consisted his merit, herein the right of his reward, the praise of his abstinence. Wherefore did he creat passions within us, pleasures round about us, but that these rightly temper'd are the very ingredients of vertue?[2]

Milton is thus putting into Eve's mouth some of his long-held beliefs. Even before the Fall, Eve exists in a world, like ours and Milton's, of temptation, but, however much assistance she has in rejecting temptation, she must face up to it. This dialectical notion, of goodness needing to face out evil in order to produce the possibility of a greater goodness, is

Milton's real justification of the 'ways of God to men' (I. 26).

Although, therefore, Adam fervently defends the justice of God's arrangements, he makes the serious qualification that, though man's condition is secure, 'within himself/The danger lies, yet lies within his power' (IX. 348–9). Man has reason, which is free but dangerously susceptible to 'some fair appearing good' which might 'misinform the will/To do what God expressly hath forbid' (IX. 354–6). Adam again advises Eve to stay, suspecting, correctly, the possibility of 'some specious object by the foe suborned (i.e. 'bribed')' which might corrupt her reason. But in the end he does not want a passively obedient Eve, any more than the creator wanted a passively obedient mankind (IX. 361; 111, 110). He makes the only reasonable decision, and says to Eve:

> *Go; for thy stay, not free, absents thee more;*
> *Go in thy native innocence, rely*
> *On what thou hast of virtue, summon all,*
> *For God towards thee hath done his part, do thine.*
>
> (IX. 372–5)

Eve has the last word, and, ominously, 'from her husband's hand her hand/Soft she withdrew' (IX. 385–6). This reminds us of Adam's waking of Eve after her disturbed sleep when he whispers to her, 'her hand soft touching' (V. 17). Their hands are to touch again in the violence of their lustful sex after the Fall, when 'her hand he seized', but they are to unite most poignantly and finally in the penultimate line of the poem. Eve promises to be back by noon, but in this she is deceived and fails, as in much greater things shortly, as noon is the hour of the Fall (IX. 739).

On Adam and Eve's first night of love, the narrator of the poem had exclaimed, 'Sleep on/Blest pair; and O yet happiest if ye seek/No happier state, and know to know no more', where the four 'no ... know ... know ... no' sounds had emphasized a resistance to the anticipated Fall (IV. 773–5). As the event now approaches, the narrator still protests:

> *O much deceived, much failing, hapless Eve,*
> *Of thy presumed return! Event perverse!*
> *Thou never from that hour in Paradise*
> *Found'st either sweet repast, or sound repose;*
> *Such ambush hid among sweet flowers and shades*
> *Waited with hellish rancour imminent*
> *To intercept thy way, or send thee back*
> *Despoiled of innocence, of faith, of bliss.*
>
> (IX. 404–11)

The split in Milton between the craving for the innocent ideal, as represented in the uncorrupted union of Adam and Eve, and the recognition of the benefits produced by the necessity for moral struggle consequent on the Fall produces the dialectical tension in *Paradise Lost* which gives the poem much of its power.

4 The Fall of Eve: IX. 412–833

The serpent is on his diabolic quest. He cannot believe his luck in finding Eve on her own. She is 'stooping' among the 'drooping' roses (the rhyme perhaps suggesting an identification), preoccupied with gently supporting them, unaware of the pathos of her own condition as 'fairest unsupported flower,/From her best prop so far, and storm so nigh' (IX. 427–33). The serpent draws nearer, and the effect of Eve's feminine innocence on Satan is stunning. He is like a Londoner on holiday:

> *As one who long in populous city pent,*
> *Where houses thick and sewers annoy the air,*
> *Forth issuing on a summer's morn to breathe*
> *Among the pleasant villages and farms*
> *Adjoined, from each thing met conceives delight,*
> *The smell of grain, or tedded* [i.e. 'spread out to dry']
> *grass, or kine* [i.e. 'cows'],
> *Or dairy, each rural sight, each rural sound.*
>
> (IX. 445–51)

But the sight of Eve surpasses all:

> *... her heavenly form*
> *Angelic, but more soft, and feminine,*
> *Her graceful innocence, her every air* [i.e. 'manner']
> *Of gesture or least action overawed*
> *His malice.*
>
> (IX. 457–61)

For a moment Satan is disoriented, though not for long:

> *That space the evil one abstracted stood*
> *From his own evil, and for the time remained*
> *Stupidly good, of enmity disarmed,*
> *Of guile, of hate, of envy, of revenge;*

> *But the hot hell that always in him burns,*
> *Though in mid heaven, soon ended his delight,*
> *And tortures him now more, the more he sees*
> *Of pleasure not for him ordained: then soon*
> *Fierce hate he recollects.*
>
> (IX. 463–71)

In another tormented soliloquy, which confirms his joy in destroying (and represses the townsman's pleasure in the sweet-smelling countryside), Satan admits his wariness of Adam's intellect, strength, courage, and physique – 'foe not informidable' he describes him (IX. 486). So the separation of the couple *was* of crucial importance. In compressed, telegraphic style, Satan's thoughts now turn to Eve. She is fair enough for gods to love, though not for gods to be in awe of, or fear, as can happen with love and beauty when it is not met with a stronger hate, such as he has:

> *She fair, divinely fair, fit love for gods,*
> *Not terrible, though terror be in love*
> *And beauty, not approached by stronger hate,*
> *Hate stronger, under show of love well feigned,*
> *The way which to her ruin now I tend.*
>
> (IX. 489–93)

Thus an erotic and aggressive undertone is given to Satan's approach to Eve, as he now describes her as 'with ravishment beheld' (IX. 541).

The serpent approaches Eve 'erect':

> *. . . on his rear,*
> *Circular base of rising folds, that towered*
> *Fold above fold a surging maze, his head*
> *Crested aloft, and carbuncle* [i.e. 'reddish'] *his eyes;*
> *With burnished neck of verdant gold, erect*
> *Amidst his circling spires, that on the grass*
> *Floated redundant: pleasing was his shape,*
> *And lovely, never since of serpent kind*
> *Lovelier.*
>
> (IX. 497–505)

The 'fold above fold a surging maze' may remind us of the fallen angels in Book II with their inconclusive philosophizing 'in wandering mazes lost', and of Sin, Satan's daughter and lover, who was fair to the waist, 'but ended foul in many a scaly fold/... a serpent armed/With mortal sting' (II. 561, 651–3). The serpent approaches obliquely, until, with greater boldness, 'admiring' and 'fawning', he attracts Eve's attention and begins to speak with his tongue (IX. 524, 526). His sycophantic words are those of a courtly lover addressing his 'sovereign mistress' as a goddess (IX. 532). He gazes 'insatiate' on her, and asks a question similar to one which Eve had earlier asked Adam (IX. 536). Eve, marvelling at the sky at night, had asked why the stars shine when they are unobserved because all creatures are asleep, and Adam had replied that 'millions of spiritual creatures walk the earth/Unseen', observing and praising God's works by day and night (IV. 677–8). Eve's question was asked in genuine inquiry about something, the night sky, which can mediate an awareness of God. Satan's question is asked with deceptive slyness, in order to draw Eve's attention from God to herself, and thus encourage her individualism, already begun in her separation from Adam. Satan contradicts his recently expressed attitude to the beauty of Paradise, as it now becomes an 'enclosure wild':

> *Fairest resemblance of thy maker fair*
> *Thee all things living gaze on ...*
> *... but here*
> *In this enclosure wild, these beasts among,*
> *Beholders rude, and shallow to discern*
> *Half what in thee is fair, one man except,*
> *Who sees thee? (And what is one?) Who shouldst be seen*
> *A goddess among gods, adored and served*
> *By angels numberless, thy daily train.*
>
> (IX. 538–48)

So Eve is tempted to conceive of herself as independent deity rather than dependent human being. The situation here is analogous to the plot of Milton's *Comus*, written in 1634, in which drama Comus uses 'well-placed words of glozing [i.e. 'flattering'] courtesy/Baited with reasons not unplausible' to attempt his seduction of the Lady (*Comus*. 161–2).

Satan's words go straight 'into the heart of Eve', thus bypassing her reason which should be her only safeguard (IX. 550). Her first reaction is to express astonishment both at the use of language by an animal and at the serpent's friendliness, but this innocence gives Satan the opening he wants to tell his seductive story. His address now promotes Eve from 'sovereign mistress' to resplendent 'empress of this fair world', and his lying story is a rags-to-riches tale in which food and taste play a crucially significant part:

I was at first as other beasts that graze
The trodden herb, of abject thoughts and low,
As was my food, nor aught but food discerned
Or sex, and apprehended nothing high:
Till on a day roving the field, I chanced
A goodly tree far distant to behold
Loaden with fruit of fairest colours mixed,
Ruddy and gold: I nearer drew to gaze;
When from the boughs a savoury odour blown,
Grateful to appetite, more pleased my sense
Than smell of sweetest fennel or the teats
Of ewe or goat dropping with milk at even,
Unsucked of lamb or kid, that tend their play.
To satisfy the sharp desire I had
Of tasting those fair apples, I resolved
Not to defer; hunger and thirst at once,
Powerful persuaders, quickened at the scent
Of that alluring fruit, urged me so keen.

(IX. 571–88)

The 'appetite' and 'sharp desire' caused by the 'savoury odour' of the 'alluring fruit' cause him to eat until 'sated', when, he claims, he could both reason and speak:

Thenceforth to speculations high or deep
I turned my thoughts, and with capacious mind
Considered all things visible in heaven,
Or earth, or middle, all things fair and good;
But all that fair and good in thy divine
Semblance, and in thy beauty's heavenly ray
United I beheld; no fair to thine
Equivalent or second, which compelled
Me thus, though importune perhaps, to come
And gaze, and worship thee of right declared
Sovereign of creatures, universal dame.

(IX. 602–12)

Eve, coyly flattered by the praise in spite of its blatant idolatry, asks where the tree is, at which he 'leading swiftly rolled/In tangles, and made intricate seem straight,/To mischief swift' (IX. 631–3). Eve is now well into an irretrievable situation: her passions, as a result of flattery, are ruling her reason, and the serpent is confusing what reason she can deploy by disguising intricate tangles of persuasive deception as simplicity for 'our credulous mother' (IX. 644). In a compelling epic simile, Satan misleads Eve like an *ignis fatuus*, or will-o'-the-wisp (a kind of phosphorescent light often seen over marshy ground, caused by the spontaneous combustion of gas from decaying material). Milton calls the effect a 'wandering fire',

> *... which the night*
> *Condenses, and the cold environs round,*
> *Kindled through agitation to a flame,*
> *Which oft, they say, some evil spirit attends*
> *Hovering and blazing with delusive light,*
> *Misleads the amazed night-wanderer from his way*
> *To bogs and mires, and oft through pond or pool,*
> *There swallowed up and lost, from succour far.*
> *So glistered the dire snake, and into fraud*
> *Led Eve our credulous mother, to the tree*
> *Of prohibition, root of all our woe.*
>
> (IX. 635–45)

The reverberating monosyllabic 'woe' echoes the opening lines of the poem, just before Eve's nervous, and ironic, pun on 'fruit' does the same: 'Serpent, we might have spared our coming hither,/Fruitless to me, though fruit be here to excess' (IX. 647–8). We anticipate here the 'fruitless hours' which will be spent in mutual accusation after the Fall (IX. 1188). The irony is that Eve's visit to the tree will not have been fruitless in the end. Eve at this point is described as 'yet sinless', so, despite her dream of this very moment in Book V, despite her earlier argument with Adam, and despite her following the serpent here 'into fraud', Milton does intend us to see Eve still as uncorrupted.

The serpent now, like a skilful orator, puts on an impassioned show of pretended reverence for the actual power of the forbidden fruit operating within him, when previously, in the words of God and Adam, it had been made clear that it was merely a 'pledge' or 'sign' of obedience, with no special intrinsic properties (III. 95; IV. 428; VIII. 325). The serpent calls the tree 'wisdom-giving' and 'mother of science', and claims that it gives him the power to 'trace the ways/Of highest agents' (IX. 679–83). He now appeals, in a deft and fast-moving speech, first to Eve's vanity again (she is now 'queen of this universe'), but then to her courage, by suggesting that eating of the fruit is a 'petty trespass' which God would surely overlook because of her courage in facing up to death in order to achieve knowledge of good and evil (IX. 684, 693). The serpent's argument is here at its most plausible – is it just to forbid knowledge of good? is not evil more easily shunned if it is known? – and, in a brilliant, condensed piece of spurious logic, he argues that her fear must actually eliminate itself:

> *God therefore cannot hurt ye, and be just;*
> *Not just, not God; not feared then, nor obeyed:*
> *Your fear it self of death removes the fear.*
>
> (IX. 700–702)

The serpent now quickly discredits God's motives in imposing the prohibition ('to keep ye low and ignorant'), suggests that death as a human will be an enhancement of their condition to that of gods (just as his own condition has apparently been enhanced from that of beast to human), and then argues that there can be nothing in knowledge ('And wherein lies/The offence, that man should thus attain to know?') (IX. 704, 725–6). This last point pushes further the drift of Eve's own earlier words to Adam, where she had asked what was virtue unless it was tested (IX. 322–6). Here the serpent asks what is wrong with *knowing*, and how can it hurt God? And this was Milton, in 1644:

> To the pure all things are pure, not only meats and drinks, but all kinds of knowledge whether of good or evill; the knowledge cannot defile, nor consequently the books, if the will and conscience be not defil'd.[3]

The crucial shift between Milton in 1644 and the serpent now is that the serpent's will is defiled. The serpent is inviting Eve to become a heroic resistance fighter against an oppressive God who wants to keep her 'low and ignorant' (though, at the same time, he is cleverly arguing that, of course, God cannot mind if she disobeys anyway). Milton in 1644 had also been a heroic verbal resistance fighter in the English Revolution. Its failure was what led him to believe that faithful obedience, such as that displayed by Abdiel in this poem, to some larger concept of man's duties and obligations to God was superior to fallible reasoning about how to bring about God's kingdom on earth through the courageous agency of elect individuals, or even the English people (V. 896–905). Obedience to the supreme authority of Providence, whose existence this poem is designed to assert, will render man invulnerable to the assaults of historical reversals, where God's plans seem to be going wrong. It is by individual struggle and testimony, such as that of Abdiel, that true virtue is to be achieved.

Innocent Eve is, of course, persuaded by the serpent, but not through ignoring reason:

> *. . . in her ears the sound*
> *Yet rung of his persuasive words, impregned*

With reason, to her seeming, and with truth.

(IX. 736–8)

She acts according to her limited reason, as she sees 'truth'. Only then does 'appetite', stimulated by the savoury smell of the fruit, make her desire to eat. It is anyway already noon, and therefore lunch-time. She addresses the fruit, as the serpent had previously addressed the tree, and summarizes his arguments to herself. She no longer trusts God, since his apparent prohibition on knowledge is a prohibition on goodness and wisdom, which is necessarily invalid. As for the threat of death, the serpent did not die, so what is there to fear? Then occurs her Fall:

So saying, her rash hand in evil hour
Forth reaching to the fruit, she plucked, she ate:
Earth felt the wound, and nature from her seat
Sighing through all her works gave signs of woe,
That all was lost. Back to the thicket slunk
The guilty serpent, and well might, for Eve
Intent now wholly on her taste, naught else
Regarded, such delight till then, as seemed,
In fruit she never tasted, whether true
Or fancied so, through expectation high
Of knowledge, nor was godhead from her thought.
Greedily she engorged without restraint,
And knew not eating death.

(IX. 780–92)

Earth is wounded, and the consequences become fully apparent shortly (X. 651–719). The word 'woe' reverberates here too. Eve is overwhelmed with greedy, unrestrained appetite, and reason is now gone since she is drunk, 'heightened as with wine' (IX. 793). She promises the tree her praise each morning, which previously had been given to God, and she refers to God in the pagan way as 'gods', or indeterminately as 'others', or as 'our great forbidder' (V. 145; IX. 804, 805, 815). She still nevertheless feels the need for secrecy, and takes some comfort in the remoteness of heaven. The big question for her is what to tell Adam, who has not figured in her thoughts since she left him. She has to decide between sharing her new 'happiness' with Adam by giving him the fruit to eat, and keeping her new condition to herself in order to 'draw his love' by ensuring her equality or even superiority to him (IX. 822). She now conceives of her mutual relationship with Adam as one of domination and servitude: she speaks for the first time of the inferiority of the female, and asks 'inferior, who is free?' (IX. 825). But then a thought strikes her: 'what if God have seen,/And death ensue?' (IX. 826–7). If this is so, the choice facing her is between dying herself, with the envious idea of Adam 'wedded to another Eve', and dying with Adam by persuading him to join her in eating the fruit (IX. 828). So she resolves, because of her love for Adam, which she explicitly states here for the first time, that she will make him share her fate, whatever it is: 'So dear I love him, that with him all deaths/I could endure, without him live no life' (IX. 832–3). This is now truly a selfish love.

5 The Fall of Adam: IX. 834–1007

Adam is looking forward to Eve's return, after the first separation of their lives. He has woven a garland of flowers for her to wear, but feels anxious at her delay, so walks to meet her. He finds her near the tree of knowledge, carrying a 'bough of fairest fruit' (IX. 851). Just as the duplicitous serpent had made his final approach to Eve partly in the metaphorical guise of an actor (note the words 'part', 'motion' [i.e. 'gesture'], 'act', 'audience', in IX. 673–4), so Eve embarrassedly speaks first to Adam, with an excuse for her delay in her face as 'prologue', and as 'prompt' for her verbal 'apology' (i.e. 'defence') (IX. 853–4).

It seems unfair to suggest that Eve is here motivated entirely by a calculation to deceive. She really believes she has acted in the best interests of herself, and by extension of Adam, since she wants to share her fate with him 'in bliss or woe' (IX. 831). We therefore can only find her statement of love for Adam poignant, though notably excessive in its passionate expression – 'agony of love', and 'pain of absence from thy sight' (IX. 858, 861). As she tells of what has happened, her intoxicated exaggerations, signalling perhaps her desperation that Adam should approve, strike an ominous note. The 'serpent wise', she says,

> *. . . with me*
> *Persuasively hath so prevailed, that I*
> *Have also tasted, and have also found*
> *The effects to correspond, opener mine eyes,*
> *Dim erst, dilated spirits, ampler heart,*
> *And growing up to godhead; which for thee*
> *Chiefly I sought, without thee can despise.*
>
> (IX. 872–8)

She concludes her excited speech by referring to the pagan concept of 'fate', as the serpent earlier had, thus implicitly denying the authority of divine providence (IX. 689, 885).

In a magnificent symbolic moment, Adam's horror is described, the flushing glow of Eve's 'distemper' contrasting with his 'horror chill' (IX. 887, 890). At this moment the roses, representing human frailty, fade – the first instance of decay in Paradise:

> *Thus Eve with countenance blithe her story told;*
> *But in her cheek distemper flushing glowed.*
> *On the other side, Adam, soon as he heard*
> *The fatal trespass done by Eve, amazed,*
> *Astonied stood and blank, while horror chill*
> *Ran through his veins, and all his joints relaxed;*
> *From his slack hand the garland wreathed for Eve*
> *Down dropped, and all the faded roses shed:*
> *Speechless he stood and pale.*
>
> (IX. 886–94)

Adam is losing his grip. We remember how he had confessed to Raphael that his love for Eve was so great that 'what she wills to do or say,/Seems wisest, virtuousest, discreetest, best', and how Raphael had advised Adam 'In loving thou dost well, in passion not,/Wherein true love consists not; love refines/The thoughts, and heart enlarges, hath his seat/In reason' (VIII. 549–50, 588–91). Adam is now shattered, and sees that Eve is 'defaced, deflowered, and now to death devote' (IX. 901). The one described as 'fairest unsupported flower' when tying up the roses is now 'deflowered' among the faded roses of Adam's garland – thus highlighting the metaphorical seduction of her virginal spiritual innocence by Satan (IX. 432).

Adam is shrewd enough to guess that Eve has been the object of 'some cursed fraud', but, having reasoned accurately, he immediately suffers a failure of the will to do right, and asserts 'Certain my resolution is to die' (IX. 904, 907). The cause is his excess of love for Eve, about which Raphael had warned, and his failure, when presented as now with a choice between human love and divine love, to choose the latter. Having earlier argued unsuccessfully against separation from Eve, Adam now finds life totally meaningless without her, and he expresses this emotion in a masterly image of existential despair:

> *How can I live without thee, how forgo*
> *Thy sweet converse and love so dearly joined,*
> *To live again in these wild woods forlorn?*

> *Should God create another Eve, and I*
> *Another rib afford, yet loss of thee*
> *Would never from my heart; no no, I feel*
> *The link of nature draw me: flesh of flesh,*
> *Bone of my bone thou art, and from thy state*
> *Mine never shall be parted, bliss or woe.*
>
> (IX. 908–16)

The reference to the marriage bond ('flesh of flesh,/Bone of my bone thou art') makes us feel not merely the passion but also the element of *rightness* in Adam's wrong choice to fall with Eve (VIII. 495–9).

It is perhaps hard for the twentieth-century reader to accept that any abstract rule of law or obedience should be allowed to break up a love-relationship. Perhaps it was less hard for the seventeenth-century reader if, as the historian Lawrence Stone argues, 'affective individualism' first developed in the seventeenth century and changed forever the nature of family relations in England. Affective individualism as defined by Stone has many facets, but he proposes that Puritanism's 'stress on the importance of holy matrimony – meaning marriage bound by mutual affection – helped to undermine its contrary emphasis on the need for strict filial obedience to parents'.[4] If this was so, Milton, and his poem, stood at this crossroads: the filial obedience required of Adam as son of God is here crossed by the mutual affection of his marriage-bond. The mention by both Eve and Adam of the idea of 'another Eve' can be seen in this light, therefore, not only as a defence of God's providence in case the first Eve should fall (so that Adam is not obliged to choose between falling himself or remaining childless), but also in their rejection of the idea, as an emphasis on the individuality and irreplaceability of Eve herself (IX. 828, 911). Milton, of course, in justifying the ways of God to men, needs to take a tough line with affective individualism – hence the felt contradiction between the love of Adam and Eve and the stern judgment of the narrative voice that Adam was 'not deceived,/But fondly overcome with female charm' (IX. 998–9).

Adam's response to Eve when he has collected his thoughts shows him slipping quickly into the ideological world of Satan. He refers, in the third and last use of the word in this book, to 'fate' as an alternative power as helpless as 'God omnipotent' to undo what has been done (IX. 927). He takes Eve's story of the serpent's having tasted the fruit to be true, and accepts the implications for their future as gods of the serpent's apparently becoming like a human. He reasons that God probably wouldn't carry out his threat of death for disobedience because the world of nature, which was created for them, would therefore also fail, and this would give the adversary the opportunity to make the scornful taunt: 'Fickle their state whom God/Most favours ... me first/He ruined, now mankind; whom will he next?' (IX. 948–50). Satan, we remember, on his first landing on earth had fortified himself against remorse with the line, 'Evil be thou my good' (IV. 110). Now Adam, in the course of a moving expression of his love for Eve, which will take him into opposition to God, articulates a similar paradox – 'death is to me as life':

> *However I with thee have fixed my lot,*
> *Certain to undergo like doom, if death*
> *Consort with thee, death is to me as life;*
> *So forcible within my heart I feel*
> *The bond of nature draw me to my own,*
> *My own in thee, for what thou art is mine;*
> *Our state cannot be severed, we are one,*
> *One flesh; to lose thee were to lose my self.*
>
> (IX. 952–9)

Eve's last words now, before Adam's fatal act, begin with ecstatic intensity at hearing his declaration of his love for her – 'O glorious trial of exceeding love,/Illustrious evidence, example high!' (IX. 961–2). Whereas in the previous book Adam had spoken of his union of *mind* and soul with Eve, here she speaks of their unity as 'one *heart*, one soul', having displaced the intellect by the passions (VIII. 604; IX. 967). Adam's willingness to die for love is a contrast with the Messiah's offer to die for mankind: above the Messiah's 'immortal love' shone his 'filial obedience', whereas Adam's filial obedience is overruled by his love for Eve (III. 267–9; IX. 975). Eve feels that his disobedience ennobles his love for her. She tenderly weeps, and then – the fatal moment:

> *She gave him of that fair enticing fruit*
> *With liberal hand: he scrupled not to eat*
> *Against his better knowledge, not deceived,*
> *But fondly overcome with female charm.*
> *Earth trembled from her entrails, as again*
> *In pangs, and nature gave a second groan,*
> *Sky loured and muttering thunder, some sad drops*
> *Wept at completing of the mortal sin*
> *Original.*
>
> (IX. 996–1004)

The first sigh of earth when Eve ate the fruit here becomes a second groan, as the first thunderstorm occurs (IX. 783). Nature is weeping. Adam has made a choice between his partner and his God, and in full knowledge made the wrong choice. The fruit offered by Eve is 'enticing', and Adam's reason is foolishly, or affectionately ('fondly' has both implications), overcome as if bewitched, or charmed.

6 Fallen Sexuality, Shame, and Recrimination: IX. 1008–1189

Adam too becomes intoxicated 'as with new wine', a feeling unknown before the Fall when there was no fermentation. He and Eve together feel that they 'swim in mirth' and that they are 'breeding wings/Wherewith to scorn the earth' – in fact becoming divine (IX. 1009–11). Carnal desire is indeed causing them to burn with lust. Here their mutual desire becomes inflamed and therefore hell-like, unlike their earlier wedded love celebrated in Book IV, and 'wantonly' takes on its fallen meaning as Eve returns Adam's lascivious look (IV. 750ff.; IX. 1013–15). Here also, in Adam's words, the central theme of 'tasting' in the poem is fully elaborated:

> *Eve, now I see thou art exact of taste,*
> *And elegant, of sapience no small part,*
> *Since to each meaning savour we apply,*
> *And palate call judicious; I the praise*
> *Yield thee, so well this day thou hast purveyed.*
> *Much pleasure we have lost, while we abstained*
> *From this delightful fruit, nor known till now*
> *True relish, tasting; if such pleasure be*
> *In things to us forbidden, it might be wished,*
> *For this one tree had been forbidden ten.*
>
> (IX. 1017–26)

(Note that 'sapience' is derived from the Latin word *sapientia*, meaning 'discernment, or taste'.) Adam's earlier reservations about Eve's 'less exact' [i.e. 'perfect'] inward qualities are now gone in his sensuous delight (VIII. 539). In a reversal of the established order, Adam praises Eve, but whereas previously she was virtuous, now he, like the fallen Eve, calls the tree 'virtuous' (IX. 795, 1033).

Their lovemaking is now not, as previously, 'chaste', but more like the 'casual fruition' of 'adulterous lust' (IV. 735, 761, 767). The result of their inflamed desire is that Adam 'seized' Eve's hand, and they 'took their fill of love and love's disport', until sleep 'oppressed them, wearied with their amorous play' (IX. 1037, 1042, 1045). Milton here echoes the words in Proverbs 7:18 of the woman 'with the attire of an harlot', who seduces a young man while her husband is away, saying 'Come, let us take our fill of love'. Also the sleep of Adam and Eve had previously been 'airy light' because it derived from 'temperate vapours bland', whereas now their sleep results from intemperate lust rather than from love, so that they rise from it 'as from unrest' (V. 4, 5; IX. 1052). They have lost the veil of innocence, together with their 'native righteousness/And honour', and have now only the robe of shame, which reveals more than it covers (IX. 1054–9). Like Samson who lost his strength, they have lost their virtue (and an early meaning of 'virtue' was 'strength', as in Chaucer), though we should remember that Adam was 'not deceived', whereas the story of Samson in Judges 16 makes it clear that he was deceived (IX. 998).

After a long, embarrassed silence, Adam's first words make an implicit punning link between Eve and evil: 'O Eve, in evil hour ...' (IX. 1067). Though he never meets Satan, Adam has now realized that the serpent has been taught by someone to 'counterfeit man's voice' (IX. 1069). The first sign of Adam and Eve's 'knowledge' of good and evil has been their lustful sexuality, and behind the use of 'know' here is the Hebraism, according to which the word means 'to have carnal acquaintance with' (IX. 1071). More significant than mere lust, however, is the resulting sense of shame at their loss of honour, innocence, faith, and purity. Since Horace, the Roman poet of the first century B.C., there has been a literary convention, a form of pastoral, which celebrates retirement to the country as an escape from the vices and corruption of urban life. Here Adam, already in the country, in an adaptation of the convention considers solitary retirement as a way of escaping from God's observation, such is his shame:

> *... O might I here*
> *In solitude live savage, in some glade*
> *Obscured, where highest woods impenetrable*
> *To star or sunlight, spread their umbrage broad*
> *And brown as evening: cover me ye pines,*
> *Ye cedars, with innumerable boughs*
> *Hide me, where I may never see them* [i.e. 'heavenly shapes' of God or angel] *more.*
>
> (IX. 1084–90)

In fact he chooses rather to hide the genitals, 'those middle parts', which are now a symbol of their shame. They choose the leaves of the banyan tree, or Indian fig, which has the characteristic that the branches hang down and take root where they touch the ground. This shady tree seems to become here a symbol of sin, since sin in the human race will proliferate with similar ease from now on. They sew and put on these large leaves, and come to resemble the American Indians found by Columbus. Their relationship is now dominated not by smiles which flow from reason and feed love, as Adam had earlier described when trying to persuade Eve not to work separately from him, but by 'high passions':

> *... not at rest or ease of mind,*
> *They sat them down to weep, nor only tears*
> *Rained at their eyes, but high winds worse within*
> *Began to rise, high passions, anger, hate,*
> *Mistrust, suspicion, discord, and shook sore*
> *Their inward state of mind, calm region once*
> *And full of peace, now tossed and turbulent:*
> *For understanding ruled not, and the will*
> *Heard not her lore, both in subjection now*
> *To sensual appetite, who from beneath*
> *Usurping over sovereign reason claimed*
> *Superior sway.*
>
> (IX. 1120–31)

The words 'usurping ... sovereign ... sway' indicate metaphorically that the Fall is a public and political matter, as well as an individual one. Insurrection and disorder will now follow at all levels – personal, political, and also natural, as the metaphor of 'high winds' implies.

'It was all your fault,' charges Adam, 'for going off on your own like that.' 'No, it could just as easily have happened to you,' responds Eve. In Milton's words – 'Was I to have never parted from thy side?/As good have grown there still a lifeless rib' (IX. 1153–4). 'Anyway, why didn't you command me not to go off? You're the head! If you'd been more firm everything would have been all right!' Adam is incensed: 'So this is your love for me, is it? I am the one who chose to die for you, remember? What was I supposed to do? I warned you about the danger, but to have forced you to stay would have overruled your free will. You thought that you would either be safe, or else have some "glorious trial" of your obedience.' Milton's words again – 'Perhaps/I also erred in overmuch admiring/What seemed in thee so perfect' (IX. 1177–9). 'My error has now become my crime. Never trust a woman: she won't be restrained and will always blame the man,' concludes Adam. Their bitter recriminations are centred on the perennial struggle between authority and freedom. Their mutuality is now 'fruitless' and self-centred:

Thus they in mutual accusation spent
The fruitless hours, but neither self-condemning,
And of their vain contest appeared no end.

(IX. 1187–9)

Human history has now begun.

7 Heaven's Judgment: X. 1–228

Following the climactic events of Book IX, as the poetic narrative draws to its close, we find in Book X a series of six separate episodes and locations revealing the varied reactions of characters we have already met: God, the Son, Sin and Death, Satan, the fallen angels, and of course Adam and Eve themselves. The tenth book is rather like a film which cuts from one place to another to show events happening at more or less the same time and to draw the strands of the plot together. The first scene is in heaven, which is introduced with a reminder of God's defence in relation to the Fall, which he made in Book III. The defence is that God is all-seeing, and gave man the free will and strength to resist Satan, but that man's disobedience must incur the inexorable penalty of death.

God, being omniscient, knows what has happened on earth, though the angels learn of it only when the angelic guards of the universe, chief of whom is Gabriel, arrive with the news (IV. 549–50; X. 18). Moved by sadness and pity, they all rush to hear what God has to say about it. Milton faces the same problems as before in making God speak to defend the apparently indefensible. The solution to the theological problem of God's apparent blame for the Fall is again a combination of divine foreknowledge and human free will, which keeps God firmly in charge, but not responsible for his creation. God predicted what would happen, but did not prevent it, because that would have been an infringement of the human pair's free will, which God 'left/In even scale' (III. 92; X. 46–47). This image of the scales we have seen already, when, at the end of Book IV, God hangs forth his golden scales in heaven, and they tip to indicate that Gabriel should not fight or detain Satan, which would have prevented him from tempting and seducing Eve. Highlighting the narrative problem faced by Milton in defending God, William Empson pertinently asks whether it is 'the uneasy conscience of God or of Milton which produces this unfortunate metaphor of the scales, actually reminding us of the incident when he forced his troops to expose mankind to the tempter?'[5] God now sends the Son to pronounce the death sentence on Adam and Eve, which Adam had hoped would not materialize (IX. 928).

By sending his Son as 'Man's friend, his mediator, his designed/Both ransom and redeemer voluntary', God can claim to be tempering justice with mercy, as he had earlier announced that he would (X. 60–61; III. 132–4). The Son accepts his mission, and arrives on earth in late afternoon (we remember that the Fall took place around noon (IX. 739)).

Immediately we notice a contrast with the arrival of the previous angelic guest in Paradise, Raphael, who arrived for lunch in Book V (V. 350–51). On that occasion Adam had walked forth to greet Raphael, but now the Son, here called God, since he is now acting as God's 'vicegerent' or authorized representative, cannot at first find Adam, and calls out 'Where art thou? ... come forth' (X. 56, 103, 108). Shamefacedly Adam and Eve appear, but 'love was not in their looks, either to God/Or to each other' (X. 111–12). God now teases them, much as he had done previously when discussing with Adam the possible need of a companion for him, and pretends that he does not know what has happened (VIII. 369–451). Adam, however, confesses the truth, and blames Eve: 'She gave me of the tree and I did eat' (X. 143). God points out that Adam has been guilty of a wrong choice of role in relation to Eve: she should have attracted his love, not his subjection, since rulership was, he says, 'thy part [i.e. 'role']/And person [i.e. 'character'], hadst thou known thy self aright' (X. 155–6). Eve, more abashed than Adam, blames the serpent.

Now follows the tripartite curse: first, the serpent, whose curse involves a hint of human redemption – 'her seed shall bruise thy head'; second, Eve, who is condemned to pain and sorrow in childbirth, and to submission to her husband's will – 'he over thee shall rule'; and finally, Adam, who is condemned to hard labour on a cursed ground 'all the days of thy life' (X. 181, 196, 202). This reminds us of the very careful wording of the penalty for disobedience in Book VIII: 'inevitably thou shalt die;/From that day mortal' (VIII. 330–31). Death is thus certain, though delayed. God now takes pity on the human pair's nakedness, and gives them clothes in the form of 'skins of beasts' – the result, possibly, of the first killings on earth (X. 217). On his return to heaven, the Son tells the Father what he has done – the Father who is 'all-knowing' anyway (X. 227).

8 A Highway to Hell: X. 229–409

The characters in this next episode, Sin and Death, the children of Satan, we last met in Book II, where, having let Satan out of hell, Sin was unable to shut the doors again (II. 883–4). What we now observe is a commentary and embellishment in another, more allegorical mode, on the Fall and judgment. The opening takes us back to earlier in the day – 'meanwhile ere thus was sinned and judged on earth' (X. 229). Sin feels sure that Satan has been successful in his mission to find earth and liberate hell, and, like Adam and Eve after their Fall, begins to feel elated. As Adam and Eve begin to 'fancy that they feel/Divinity within them breeding wings', so likewise Sin feels 'new strength within me rise,/Wings growing' (IX. 1009–10; X. 243–4). And just as Adam, after Eve has eaten the fruit, feels an intuitive misgiving, so Sin feels a 'sympathy, or some connatural force' linking her with Satan (IX. 845–6; X. 246). She proposes a project, a kind of parody of the creation, which is to build a permanent bridge from hell to the universe, 'a monument/Of merit high to all the infernal host' (X. 258–9). Death, who is her son and Satan's son, a 'meagre shadow' (i.e. 'skeleton'), using the pagan language of 'fate' as Sin had of 'lot', reassures her of his support, since he can 'taste/The savour of death' from earth (X. 261, 265, 268–9). This reminds us tragically of Eve's greedy eating of the fruit 'and knew not eating death', and of the reverberation of the words 'taste' and 'savour', at this point bitterly ironic, through the poem (IX. 792; X. 268, 269).

Like 'ravenous fowl', Sin and Death fly out of hell into the surrounding Chaos and make a solid bridge of prodigious length from hell to the point on the universe at which Satan had first landed when he had escaped from hell (X. 274; III. 418–22; X. 315–16). This will provide a 'broad,/Smooth, easy' passage down to hell (X. 304–5). Milton's anti-catholic pun here – 'wondrous art/Pontifical' (the Pope's title is 'pontifex maximus', meaning 'bridge-builder', but to heaven) – is really a side-issue: the bridge is fastened to the universe 'with pins of adamant [i.e. 'very hard', and probably with a pun on 'Adam']/And chains', which is a parody of the 'golden chain' from which the universe hangs from heaven (X. 312–13, 318–19; II. 1051). The bridge to hell now obstructs the passage from earth to heaven, just as Arctic icebergs 'stop the imagined way' to Cathay, or, by implication, as fallen human nature prevents access to Paradise (III. 528; X. 291).

Satan is now observed in the disguise of 'an angel bright' (X. 327). He has observed Adam's Fall, but fled when the Son came to pass judgment. Though he has now understood the implications for himself of the curse on the serpent, he is nevertheless overjoyed at the success of his mission, and even more at the sight of the 'stupendous bridge' (X. 351). Sin addresses Satan as the 'author and prime architect' of the edifice, names previously applied to God himself (V. 73, 256). She continues:

> *Thine now is all this world, thy virtue hath won*
> *What thy hands builded not, thy wisdom gained*

With odds what war hath lost, and fully avenged
Our foil in heaven; here thou shalt monarch reign,
There didst not; there let him still victor sway,
As battle hath adjudged, from this new world
Retiring, by his own doom alienated,
And henceforth monarchy with thee divide.

(X. 372–9)

Satan is confident in having made 'one realm/Hell and this world, one realm, one continent/Of easy thoroughfare', and, in a parody of God's commission to Adam – 'all the earth/To thee and to thy race I give; as lords/Possess it' (VIII. 338–40) – Satan gives Sin and Death his infernal commission:

There [i.e. 'in Paradise'] *dwell and reign in bliss, thence on the earth*
Dominion exercise and in the air,
Chiefly on man, sole lord of all declared,
Him first make sure your thrall, and lastly kill.

(X. 399–402)

Satan has kept his promise (II. 840–44).

9 Satan's Accolade: X. 410–584

Hell is tense with expectation of Satan's return. Like Odysseus, the epic hero who returned home after a long journey dressed as a tattered castaway and lived with his swineherd in disguise in order to discover how things were with his family, so Satan enters hell, having travelled down the new causeway, disguised as a 'plebeian angel militant' (X. 442).[6] He then invisibly ascends his throne in Pandaemonium, until 'as from a cloud his fulgent [i.e. 'resplendent'] head/And shape star bright appeared' (X. 449–50). This is an obvious parodic echo of the Father's presence on his 'throne supreme' speaking from his 'secret cloud' which opened the book, and it also serves to emphasize the enormous change which is about to befall Satan (X. 28, 32).

Satan begins his last speech to his followers with the formal address, 'Thrones, dominations, princedoms, virtues, powers' – a list of rankings very similar to that in the Bible in the verse in which Paul attributes to the Son the agency of creation:

For by him were all things created, that are in heaven and that are in earth, visible and invisible, whether they be thrones, or dominions, or principalities, or powers: all things were created by him and for him.

(Colossians 1:16)

It is the same series of rankings as that used by God at the Exaltation of the Son in Book V, the act which first prompted Satan's rebellion, and which Satan had questioned at his royal seat in the north (V. 601):

> *Thrones, dominations, princedoms, virtues, powers,*
> *If these magnific titles yet remain*
> *Not merely titular, since by decree*
> *Another now hath to himself engrossed*
> *All power, and us eclipsed.*
>
> (V. 772–6)

Now, following the success of his mission, Satan feels that these 'magnific titles' are rightfully secured:

> *Thrones, dominations, princedoms, virtues, powers,*
> *For in possession such, not only of right,*
> *I call ye and declare ye now, returned*
> *Successful beyond hope, to lead ye forth*
> *Triumphant out of this infernal pit*
> *Abominable, accursed, the house of woe,*
> *And dungeon of our tyrant: now possess,*
> *As lords, a spacious world, to our native heaven*
> *Little inferior, by my adventure hard*
> *With peril great achieved.*
>
> (X. 460–69)

The success of the mission projected in Book II now seems fully assured, as Satan proceeds to describe the task he has accomplished as hero of his own epic story. His rhetorical gifts are here fully evident. There are exaggerations: 'Night and Chaos wild,/That jealous of their secrets fiercely opposed/My journey strange' (X. 477–9) – in fact Chaos helped him (II. 1004–9); and there is insulting mockery:

> *... him by fraud I have seduced*
> *From his creator, and the more to increase*
> *Your wonder, with an apple; he thereat*
> *Offended, worth your laughter, hath given up*
> *Both his beloved man and all this world,*
> *To Sin and Death a prey, and so to us.*
>
> (X. 485–90)

Finally, God's judgment on himself he disdainfully disparages: 'A world who would not purchase with a bruise?' (X. 500).

Now follows one of the most memorable scenes in the poem, as the expected ovation turns horribly wrong:

> *So having said, a while he stood, expecting*
> *Their universal shout and high applause*
> *To fill his ear, when contrary he hears*
> *On all sides, from innumerable tongues*
> *A dismal universal hiss, the sound*
> *Of public scorn; he wondered, but not long*
> *Had leisure, wondering at himself now more;*
> *His visage drawn he felt to sharp and spare,*
> *His arms clung to his ribs, his legs entwining*
> *Each other, till supplanted down he fell*
> *A monstrous serpent on his belly prone,*
> *Reluctant* [i.e. 'struggling'], *but in vain, a greater power*
> *Now ruled him, punished in the shape he sinned,*
> *According to his doom: he would have spoke,*
> *But hiss for hiss returned with forked tongue*
> *To forked tongue, for now were all transformed*
> *Alike, to serpents all as accessories*
> *To his bold riot: dreadful was the din*
> *Of hissing through the hall, thick swarming now*
> *With complicated monsters head and tail.*
>
> (X. 504–23)

Satan the supplanter is 'supplanted', and becomes a mere monster in God's epic at the moment that he is about to celebrate his heroic triumph in his own epic. The innocent serpent into which Satan entered has now multiplied into a snake-pit of 'dire' and 'drear' evil, and all the political deliberations of the Council in Book II have been transformed, not into a triumphant achievement, but to a 'din/Of hissing'. Outside, the waiting devils are likewise transformed, as the 'great consulting peers' emerge (X. 456):

> *. . . horror on them fell,*
> *And horrid sympathy; for what they saw,*
> *They felt themselves now changing; down their arms,*
> *Down fell both spear and shield, down they as fast,*
> *And the dire hiss renewed, and the dire form*
> *Catched by contagion, like in punishment,*
> *As in their crime.*
>
> (X. 539–45)

They now suffer the extremes of 'scalding thirst and hunger fierce', and greedily eat the fruit of trees like the fatal one in Paradise, only to find that it turns to 'bitter ashes' in their mouths, in fulfilment of the curse on the serpent that he would eat dust all the days of his life (X. 556, 566, 178). Eventually they return to their former shapes, but some say they are forced to submit to an 'annual humbling' by returning to the state of serpents, as a perpetual reminder and punishment (X. 576).

10 Nature Corrupted: X. 585–719

Meanwhile, in Paradise, Sin and the skeletal Death are beginning to celebrate their new empire by spreading 'waste and havoc' (X. 585, 617). The pervasive imagery of eating and taste continues as Death complains that there is all too little 'to stuff this maw' (i.e. 'mouth' or 'stomach'), while his mother Sin in reponse promises to infect mankind and thus 'season him thy last and sweetest prey' (X. 601, 609). Further, God observing them defends himself against the scorn of his enemies who laugh at him on account of their apparently easy victory in capturing earth, with more extreme metaphors:

> *... I called and drew them thither*
> *My hell-hounds, to lick up the draff and filth*
> *Which man's polluting sin with taint hath shed*
> *On what was pure, till crammed and gorged, nigh burst*
> *With sucked and glutted offal, at one sling*
> *Of thy victorious arm, well-pleasing Son,*
> *Both Sin, and Death, and yawning grave at last*
> *Through chaos hurled, obstruct the mouth of hell*
> *For ever, and seal up his ravenous jaws.*
>
> (X. 629–37)

The 'greedy engorging' of Eve as she ate the forbidden fruit is here escalated to an image of carnivorous gormandizing on the part of Sin and Death until the jaws of hell itself are sealed for ever. The tough message of the poem is that this horrifying decree by God (they are *his* hell-hounds) is immediately praised by the heavenly audience: 'Just are thy ways,/Righteous are thy decrees on all thy works' (X. 643–4). This is without doubt the worst of the 'ways of God to men' which Milton set out to justify. The justification seems to be that in the end good comes of it, that the Fall was 'fortunate'.

Nature itself is fundamentally affected. The symmetrical universe of before the Fall, where it was 'eternal spring' and day and night were equal because the earth was not inclined on its axis, becomes disjointed, and seasonal change together with extremes of 'cold and heat/Scarce tolerable' is introduced (IV. 268; X. 653–4, 677–8). (Milton carefully avoids a commitment here to earth-centred or sun-centred views of the universe by the strategic use of a 'some say . . . some say . . .' device (X. 668, 671).) Violent storms now begin to occur in inanimate nature, but, worse, animate nature becomes aggressively carnivorous:

> *Beast now with beast gan war, and fowl with fowl,*
> *And fish with fish; to graze the herb all leaving,*
> *Devoured each other; nor stood much in awe*
> *Of man, but fled him, or with countenance grim*
> *Glared on him passing: these were from without*
> *The growing miseries, which Adam saw*
> *Already in part, though hid in gloomiest shade,*
> *To sorrow abandoned, but worse felt within,*
> *And in a troubled sea of passion tossed.*
>
> (X. 710–18)

Adam, intimately connected with nature still, feels the internal storms of passion more powerfully than external miseries.

11 Remorse: X. 720–1104

Adam now struggles with himself to reason through what has happened and what it all means, and to understand God's 'justice' in it all. His soliloquy shows a movement towards admission that he has sinned. Milton recognized four psychological stages of repentance: recognition of sinfulness, contrition, confession, and abandonment of evil and conversion to good.[7] Adam, however, unable to feel contrition or remorse, falls into despair.

We find the fallen Adam, rather as we found the fallen Satan at the start of the poem, in darkness. Adam is tossed in a 'troubled sea of passion' and hiding from the face of God (X. 718, 723). His everyday actions of eating and drinking, together with the future prospect of begetting children, seem only to increase the curse he is under by perpetuating his life in himself or in his descendants. Did I ask to be born? he says. Justice might demand that he be returned to dust, but, he asks, 'why hast thou added/The sense of endless woes? Inexplicable/Thy justice seems' (X. 753–755). Adam is not yet contrite, and is arguing similarly to Satan, who, soliloquizing in Book IV, had questioned his own origins. Satan had argued that it would have been better if he had been created 'some inferior angel' who would then not have been ambitious, and he went on to curse God's love, which, to him, he felt, 'deals eternal woe' (IV. 59, 70).

But another voice speaks within Adam – the voice of the contract lawyer. He accepted the terms (of life) at the time he was created, so, he asks himself, 'wilt thou enjoy the good,/Then cavil the conditions?' (X. 758–9). In the language of law, he 'submits' that God's 'doom [i.e. 'judgment'] is fair' (X. 769). The penalty had been that 'the day thou eat'st thereof/... inevitably thou shalt die', so why was he still alive (VIII. 329–30)? He would now gladly die, for then at least he would be safe, but what if he could not entirely die, but a 'soul' were to survive the body (X. 783)? He (with Milton) rejects this idea, but still worries, like Belial in the council meeting, that death might not be a simple end to it all. Belial had asked:

> *Will he, so wise, let loose at once his ire,*
> *Belike through impotence, or unaware,*
> *To give his enemies their wish, and end*
> *Them in his anger, whom his anger saves*
> *To punish endless?*
>
> (II. 155–9)

So Adam worries:

> *... But say*
> *That death be not one stroke, as I supposed,*
> *Bereaving sense, but endless misery*
> *From this day onward, which I feel begun*
> *Both in me, and without me, and so last*
> *To perpetuity; ay me, that fear*
> *Comes thundering back with dreadful revolution*
> *On my defenceless head.*
>
> (X. 808–15)

Here perhaps we can hear Milton pondering the great issues of the failed English Revolution: 'why should all mankind/For one man's fault thus guiltless be condemned,/If guiltless?' (X. 822–4). 'If' guiltless. That is the question, for, in logic, only corruption can derive from the first corrupt man. Adam, with Milton, now feels forced to acknowledge God to be just, after seemingly endless maze-like reasonings such as those in which, we recall, some of the fallen angels were lost (II. 561):

> *... Him after all disputes*
> *Forced I absolve: all my evasions vain,*

And reasonings, though through mazes, lead me still
But to my own conviction: first and last
On me, me only, as the source and spring
Of all corruption, all the blame lights due;
So might the wrath.

(X. 828–34)

But this is still an intellectual response only. Adam is merely plunged into despair, 'from deep to deeper', as he considers himself similar to Satan in his crime and his punishment (X. 841, 844). God, however, had made a crucial distinction between Satan and mankind with regard to their punishment:

The first sort [i.e. the angels] *by their own suggestion fell,*
Self-tempted, self-depraved: man falls deceived
By the other first: man therefore shall find grace,
The other none.

(III. 129–32)

There is therefore some hope which Adam does not yet realize.

While Adam continues to curse his creation 'outstretched' on the ground, Eve approaches to comfort him with 'soft words', only to receive a blast of anti-feminist diatribe (X. 851, 865). 'Out of my sight, thou serpent', he begins, and accuses her of being 'but a show', 'a rib/Crooked by nature', and a 'fair defect/Of nature' (X. 867, 883–5, 891–2). He even blames God for creating woman for earth, rather than sticking to the masculine-only policy, as in heaven (X. 892–3). The catalogue which follows, of the problems which choosing a marriage-partner can make for a man, is exhaustive almost to the point of being comical:

... For either
He never shall find out fit mate, but such
As some misfortune brings him, or mistake,
Or whom he wishes most shall seldom gain
Through her perverseness, but shall see her gained
By a far worse, or if she love, withheld
By parents, or his happiest choice too late
Shall meet, already linked and wedlock-bound
To a fell adversary, his hate or shame:
Which infinite calamity shall cause
To human life, and household peace confound.

(X. 898–908)

If there is any autobiographical element in this passage relating to Milton's own problems in this regard, it is well covered with Adam's despairing exaggeration. But Eve's reaction, who 'with tears that ceased not flowing,/And tresses all disordered, at his feet/Fell humble, and embracing them, besought/His peace', might well remind us of an episode in the account of Milton's life by his nephew Edward Phillips (X. 910–13). Milton had married his first wife, Mary Powell, in 1642, but within two months she had left him, and refused to return, possibly, Phillips conjectured, because the Powells were a Royalist family and 'began to repent them of having married the eldest daughter of the family to a person so contrary to them in opinion'. Three years later, however, in 1645, when the King's cause was in decline, the family arranged a surprise meeting between Milton and his wife at the house of a relation of Milton's, where, Phillips writes,

> on a sudden he [i.e. Milton] was surprised to see one whom he thought to have never seen more, making submission and begging pardon on her knees before him; he might probably at first make some shew of aversion and rejection; but partly his own generous nature, more inclinable to reconciliation than to perseverance in anger and revenge; and partly the strong intercession of friends on both sides, soon brought him to an act of oblivion, and a firm league of peace for the future.[8]

Eve now, in an emotional and loving speech, admits her wrong and asks Adam's forgiveness. Just as Adam had exclaimed, at the moment of his intellectual acknowledgement of his conviction of sin, 'On me, me only, as the source and spring/Of all corruption, all the blame lights due', so here Eve echoes the repeated 'me' to take them one stage further – into contrition. She asks that the sentence of death 'may light/On me, sole cause to thee of all this woe,/Me me only just object of his ire' (X.832–3, 934–6). Eve weeps, and Adam relents at the sight of her, 'creature so fair his reconcilement seeking' (X. 943):

> *But rise, let us no more contend, nor blame*
> *Each other, blamed enough elsewhere, but strive*
> *In offices of love, how we may lighten*
> *Each other's burden in our share of woe.*
>
> (X. 958–61)

Adam and Eve are now united with each other, and attempting through mutal love to reduce the misery which they accept as their due, since there is still the possibility of 'a long day's dying' ahead (X. 964). In other words, they recognize God's justice, but not yet his mercy (III. 407). Eve proposes two strategies to relieve their 'extremes': one is to refrain from having children, and thus restrict the spread of misery and death, and the other is to commit suicide, if the strain of abstinence from 'nuptial embraces sweet' is too difficult, thus cutting short their own misery (X. 976, 989, 994, 1001–2). Adam, still Eve's intellectual guide, begins now to rise from their combined despair, turning to 'better hopes' (X. 1011). It is wrong, he feels, to attempt to evade God's penalty: that will only provoke him further. Their real hope is in the reference to Eve's seed bruising the serpent's head. On the positive side, he calculates, first, they are not yet dead; second, Eve's foretold pain in childbearing would doubtless be 'recompensed with joy'; and, third, his own curse, to have to earn his bread with hard labour is not so bad – 'what harm? Idleness had been worse' (X. 1052, 1055). Further, the Son out of pity had clothed them with skins of beasts, so it is likely that he would further teach them 'remedy or cure/To evils which our own misdeeds have wrought' (X. 216–17, 1079–1080). The human arts and crafts, or technology, were commonly thought to have resulted from the Fall, as a means of repairing the damage caused by it. Central to them all was the use of fire: we remember that up till now Adam and Eve had eaten cold food, and were 'guiltless of fire' (V. 396; IX. 392). Now Adam foresees the possibility of fire, 'which might supply the sun', together with other comforts which will help 'to pass commodiously this life' (X. 1078, 1083). He therefore proposes not despair, not trying to frustrate God's judgment, but rather a reliance on his mercy, which word occurs here for the first time in their conversation. They then fall to the ground with *contrite* hearts, the second stage in repentance, and *confess* their faults, the third stage, 'Departure from evil and conversion to good' is the long hard struggle remaining, the solitary lot of the true puritan. Thus Milton justifies the ways of God to men by portraying an example of solitary self-examination, without despair or anger, supported by a like-minded partner, as the true model of behaviour, in contrast to Satan's bitter, destructive vanity.

VI The Fifth Day: Paradise Lost and the Consequences

1 The Son's Intercession and Michael's Arrival in Paradise: XI. 1–369

Having left Adam and Eve 'prostrate' in humble confession at the end of Book X, now, at the start of Book XI, we find that they 'repentant stood' in prayer (X. 1099; XI. 1). The rising movement implied in this transition is now the theme of the last two books of the poem, which, in the original ten-book version of the poem published in 1667, were one book, the longest. These books contain a preview of human history as described in the Old Testament, looking forward always to Christ's sacrifice, which had been promised in Book III and implied in the sentence of punishment after the Fall (III. 241; X. 181).

Adam and Eve are now 'regenerate', and their prayers fly unimpeded to heaven, where the Son intercedes on their behalf with the Father (XI. 5). The dominant imagery of the poem is here once more brought into play, but transformed: the 'fruit' and 'savour' are now benevolent as a result of the contrition of the human pair, and are actually 'more pleasing' than unfallen man could have produced (cf. V. 83–4; IX. 741). The Son says:

> *See Father, what first fruits on earth are sprung*
> *From thy implanted grace in man, these sighs*
> *And prayers, which in this golden censer, mixed*
> *With incense, I thy priest before thee bring,*
> *Fruits of more pleasing savour from thy seed*
> *Sown with contrition in his heart, than those*
> *Which his own hand manuring* [i.e. 'cultivating'] *all the trees*
> *Of Paradise could have produced, ere fallen*
> *From innocence.*
>
> (XI. 22–30)

He goes on to plead that his forthcoming redemption of mankind will allow them to become 'one with me as I with thee am one', which reminds us of the previous references to an expected perfect and final state of existence when there will be no need for authority, since 'God shall be all in all' (XI. 44; III. 340–41; VI. 732–3).

Milton, facing his usual problem in reporting conversations with God (that, since he is omniscient, no one can tell him anything he does not already know), has God comment that the Son's request was his decree anyway (XI. 47). Now, from the new perspective of mankind's redemption, death is presented not as a punishment but as a 'remedy', preventing the possibility of immortal misery, and providing an entry into a second life for the just (XI. 62). God then summons Michael, the prince of the celestial armies, to expel Adam and Eve from Paradise, though without terrifying them, to set up a flaming sword to protect the tree of life, and to reveal the future to them – in particular the story of the woman's seed which would eventually bruise the head of the serpent, or Satan (XI. 116). The word 'seed' in this connection occurs eighteen times in Books XI and XII of *Paradise Lost*, after only six occurrences in Book X, and is a sign of the positive upward movement of the poem: the 'fruit' brought death but the 'seed' will bring life from that death. It is also worth noting that Michael, with his experience of failure to win the War in Heaven before the Son took charge, will be instructing Adam about gaining his victory on earth: the shrewdest understanding, for Michael or Milton, arises out of failure (VI. 693–5).

Adam, after a night of prayer, still is not certain of his fate, and begins to feel, as he tells Eve, that 'the bitterness of death/Is past, and we shall live', having moved from his earlier despair to a groundless optimism (XI. 157–8). He has yet to learn, from Michael, the precise balance of 'justice' and 'mercy' in God's sentence. As the last morning of the poem dawns, Eve humbly responds with an expression of her loyalty to Adam, and encouragingly tries to make the best of their new situation of arduous labour: 'Here let us live, though in fallen state, content' (XI. 180). However, in accordance with the puritan view shared by Milton that portents in the natural world could be read as 'signs' reflecting human moral behaviour, nature now gives signs to show that the human pair's expectations that things will be more or less the same, with the addition of hard labour and pain in childbirth, are seriously wrong.[1] There is a solar eclipse, an eagle pursues two other birds, and a lion hunts a hart and a hind, signalling the end of peaceful co-existence on earth, the prey of the lion providing an obvious correspondence with Adam and Eve. The peaceful lion of Paradise has now become an aggressive beast of prey (IV. 343). From the west appears a radiant white light, ending the darkness of the eclipse, but Adam, now frightened of heavenly visitors ('doubt/And carnal fear that day dimmed Adam's eye'), cannot appreciate its full glory (XI. 211–12). The contrast with the arrival of Raphael in Book V is striking. Then Adam courteously and confidently spoke first to welcome the guest, but now Adam fears that his visitor, though not 'terrible', is not 'sociably mild' like Raphael, and he asks Eve to retire from the scene

(V. 361ff.; X. 233–4). Michael, having come in part to tell of fallen human history, comes appropriately in the shape of a man, 'as man/Clad to meet man', rather than as an angel with wings, like Raphael (XI. 239–40). He speaks first, giving the sentence of delayed death and expulsion from Paradise. The effect on Adam is momentous: at the news he 'heart-strook [i.e. 'struck'] with chilling gripe [i.e. 'grip'] of sorrow stood' (XI. 264). Eve's response, from her hiding-place, is immediate and moving. The pastoral nostalgia in her speech is part of that tradition of yearning for a lost innocence that has played such a significant role in our literature:[2]

> *Must I thus leave thee Paradise? Thus leave*
> *Thee native soil, these happy walks and shades,*
> *Fit haunt of gods? Where I had hope to spend,*
> *Quiet though sad, the respite of that day*
> *That must be mortal to us both. O flowers,*
> *That never will in other climate grow,*
> *My early visitation, and my last*
> *At even, which I bred up with tender hand*
> *From the first opening bud, and gave ye names,*
> *Who now shall rear ye to the sun, or rank*
> *Your tribes, and water from the ambrosial fount?*
> *Thee lastly nuptial bower, by me adorned*
> *With what to sight or smell was sweet; from thee*
> *How shall I part, and whither wander down*
> *Into a lower world, to* [i.e. 'compared to'] *this obscure*
> *And wild, how shall we breathe in other air*
> *Less pure, accustomed to immortal fruits?*
>
> (XI. 269–85)

The last words provide a sadly ironical gloss on the first two lines of the poem, where it is clear that the 'fruit' had a 'mortal taste' rather than an immortal.

By contrast, Adam's reaction is a humble submission, followed by a different sort of regret:

> *This most afflicts me, that departing hence,*
> *As from his face I shall be hid, deprived*
> *His blessed countenance; here I could frequent,*
> *With worship, place by place where he vouchsafed*
> *Presence divine, and to my sons relate;*
> *On this mount he appeared; under this tree*
> *Stood visible, among these pines his voice*

I heard, here with him at this fountain talked:
So many grateful altars I would rear
Of grassy turf, and pile up every stone
Of lustre from the brook, in memory,
Or monument to ages, and thereon
Offer sweet smelling gums and fruits and flowers:
In yonder nether world where shall I seek
His bright appearances, or footstep trace?

(XI. 315–29)

Adam is here guilty of religious error in proposing the possible establishment of 'magical' sacred places. The Protestant religion had tried to eliminate those sacred locations which the medieval church had adapted from pagan worship. The historian Keith Thomas refers to 'the ancient worship of wells, trees, and stones', such as Adam seems keen on, and comments:

> Extreme Protestants reacted against the surviving popish traditions which seemed to attach holy qualities to material things – days of the week, patches of ground, parts of the church ... By depreciating the miracle-working aspects of religion and elevating the importance of the individual's faith in God, the Protestant Reformation helped to form a new concept of religion itself... The individual stood in a direct relationship to God and was solely dependent upon his omnipotence.[3]

Michael therefore benignly admonishes Adam for his reactionary error: God is everywhere, he explains, 'his omnipresence fills/Land, sea, and air, and every kind that lives', and so he is equally to be found outside Paradise, so long as one can identify the 'sign' of his operation (XI. 336–7, 351). As he later observes, 'God attributes to place/No sanctity' (XI. 836–7). In order to help Adam to understand and recognize the operation of God's goodness and love, he, Michael, has come to show the future, which is the story of 'supernal grace contending/With sinfulness of men' (XI. 359–60). The lesson to be learned – the lesson of the whole poem, the assertion of eternal providence, the lesson of the 1650s which Milton was attempting to make sense of – was this:

... to learn
True patience, and to temper joy with fear
And pious sorrow, equally inured
By moderation either state to bear,
Prosperous or adverse: so shalt thou lead
Safest thy life, and best prepared endure
Thy mortal passage when it comes.

(XI. 360–66)

This patience is not the 'stubborn patience' of the fallen angels in Book

II, but is the attitude identified in religious terminology as 'faith', which is the underlying theme of the rest of the poem, now that repentance has been achieved (II. 569).

2 Adam's Visions of History, to After the Flood: XI. 370–901

Having put Eve to sleep, Michael takes Adam to the highest hill of Paradise, from where it would later have been possible to see all the kingdoms of Asia, Africa, and Europe – all the known world. He then clears Adam's eyes with herbs, and shows him the effects of his 'original crime' in six separate scenes depicting the future, rather as Virgil in the *Aeneid*, Book VI, had provided a vision of the future of Rome (XI. 424). Milton paraphrases biblical history, pointing up the religious and moral lessons in order to confirm Adam's faith by teaching the 'true patience' necessary for endurance, and the need for individual integrity in the presence of murder, cruelty, self-indulgence, and ridicule (XI. 355). The scenes are like a kind of silent movie: to each of the scenes except the last Adam makes a 'wrong' response, which is corrected by Michael, so our interest is as much in the educative effect of the scenes on the audience, the fallen Adam, as in the 'movie' itself. Milton in these scenes justifies the 'miltonic' values of individual endurance and integrity in the face of adversity, which, having displayed them himself as he observed the disintegration of the idealism of the English Revolution at the end of the 1650s, he came to regard so highly. All was not lost, for Milton as for Adam: but there was a crucial shift necessary for both of them, from public esteem to private endurance.

The first scene portrays the murder by one of Adam's future sons, Cain, of his brother Abel. Cain casually selects a vegetable sacrifice, 'unculled, as came to hand', while Abel picks the 'choicest and best' of his lambs, and is killed as a result of Cain's jealous rage (XI. 436, 438). Adam's response is to criticize God's justice in allowing Abel's death – 'Is piety thus and pure devotion paid?' – but Michael shows this to be an inappropriate response, since Abel's faith will 'lose no reward' (XI. 452, 459). Now Adam has seen death for the first time, the result of sin, and he is revolted by it.

The second scene moves indoors to show a 'lazar-house', or hospital, where various forms of physical suffering brought on through 'intemperance' are shown, a result of the 'inabstinence' of Eve (XI. 472, 476):

> *Immediately a place*
> *Before his eyes appeared, sad, noisome, dark,*

A lazar-house it seemed, wherein were laid
Numbers of all diseased, all maladies
Of ghastly spasm, or racking torture, qualms
Of heart-sick agony, all feverous kinds,
Convulsions, epilepsies, fierce catarrhs,
Intestine stone and ulcer, colic pangs,
Demoniac frenzy, moping melancholy
And moon-struck madness, pining atrophy,
Marasmus [i.e. 'wasting away'], *and wide-wasting pestilence,*
Dropsies, and asthmas, and joint-racking rheums.
Dire was the tossing, deep the groans, despair
Tended the sick busiest from couch to couch;
And over them triumphant death his dart
Shook, but delayed to strike, though oft invoked
With vows, as their chief good and final hope.

(XI. 477–93)

This gruesome sight causes Adam to weep, but upon regaining his composure his judgment is once again shown by Michael to be implicitly wrong. Adam adopts a 'false' stoicism, arguing that if this is what the fallen human condition holds in store it might be better to refuse life altogether, or beg to lay it down early, and he comments that such deformities as he has seen debase God's own image in mankind (XI. 504–511). Michael's retort is that such suffering results from 'ungoverned appetite', such as Eve displayed, and that therefore God is not responsible (XI. 517). The golden rule for mankind is a counsel of moderation – 'the rule of not too much' – which will allow a death in old age, like 'ripe fruit' dropping to earth (XI. 531, 535). This is the fruit of eating the fruit. Old age, however, is never attractive: it entails a change to 'withered weak and gray', with failing senses and no 'taste of pleasure' (XI. 540, 541). Thus is brought to a climax the theme of fruit and tasting, which has been central to the poem since its first two lines. Adam makes his third error of judgment in response to this picture of old age, which is to resolve to find the easiest way to get through life with least trouble, 'and patiently attend/My dissolution' (XI. 551–2). This is 'false' patience, a passive concern with the self, and Milton added these five words in the second edition of the poem, presumably to emphasize the point of error. It is rebuked by Michael in aphoristic style:

Nor love thy life, nor hate; but what thou livest
Live well, how long or short permit to heaven.

(XI. 553–4)

The third scene is, by contrast, a panoramic landscape of tent-dwellers, the descendants of Cain (through Lamech, his great-great-great-grandson and the father of Noah), who were nomadic herdsmen, musicians and metalworkers, as described in Genesis 4:19–22. As Adam watches, the descendants of Cain's brother Seth, who seem to be just and righteous men, come down from the neighbouring hills where they live and, amid much feasting and music, marry the daughters of Lamech. Adam is greatly cheered by this, compared with the previous scenes, and observes that 'here nature seems fulfilled' (XI. 602). This is, of course, again the wrong assessment. What Adam has not correctly judged is that the women in the scene are in 'wanton dress', their eyes 'rove without rein', they marry 'all in heat', and they invoke the pagan god of marriage, Hymen (XI. 583, 586, 589, 591). The men are, in fact, 'in the amorous net/Fast caught' (XI. 586–7). Michael's stern admonition to Adam is: 'Judge not what is best/By pleasure' (XI. 603–4). The 'arts that polish life' are frequently the accomplishment of people who are 'unmindful of their maker' (and hence culture, and many forms of pleasure, have always constituted a problem for the puritan conscience) (XI. 610, 611). The 'fair atheists' of the plain were in fact 'empty of all good', Michael explains, and, in a grim joke, he comments that though they now 'swim in joy', they would soon 'swim at large' – in the impending Flood (XI. 616, 625, 626). Adam immediately makes yet another wrong judgment, in blaming Eve with a (commonplace) pun on 'woe/man' and 'woman':

> *But still I see the tenor of man's woe*
> *Holds on the same, from woman to begin.*
>
> (XI. 632–3)

That observation is swiftly rebuked, though for its implication of a diminishment of male responsibility, rather than by the assertion of equality: man 'should better hold his place/By wisdom, and superior gifts received' (XI. 635–6).

In the fourth scene, people are no longer living in tents but in towns and cities, and their whole concern is with war – despoiling the land, killing, besieging a city, meeting in war council. When a middle-aged man rises to speak to the council of 'right and wrong,/Of justice, of religion, truth, and peace,/And judgment from above', he is almost 'seized with violent hands' were it not for a cloud which descends and snatches him away (XI. 666–9). This is Enoch, whose story is briefly told in the Bible, and whose 'translation' so that he did 'not see death' was widely regarded as an analogue for the resurrection.[4] Adam weeps again at this scene, and

Michael's response comes closer to a specific description of the miltonic way in a fallen world, where 'infinite/Manslaughter' is held to be 'the highest pitch/Of human glory' (XI. 692–4). This was a world such as Milton had known: in his sonnet to Fairfax, Commander-in-Chief of Cromwell's army, written in August 1648 after a series of brilliant victories over the Royalists which was to climax in the success of the siege of Colchester later that month, he had written:

O yet a nobler task awaits thy hand;
For what can war, but endless war still breed,
Till truth, and right from violence be freed.

Likewise Michael holds up for emulation the example of Enoch, who, like Abdiel earlier in the poem, was a solitary voice for righteousness and peace against war:

The only righteous in a world perverse,
And therefore hated, therefore so beset
With foes for daring single to be just,
And utter odious truth, that God would come
To judge them with his saints.

(XI. 701–5; cf. V. 896–903)

The fifth scene returns us to 'luxury and riot, feast and dance,/Marrying or prostituting' (XI. 715–16). This is the world before the Flood, and the people are so intent on their self-indulgence that they ignore the warnings by Noah of imminent judgment. Noah's world, like Adam's, was lost because of sin. With a combination of features from Genesis, chapters 6–8, and from Ovid's story of Deucalion's flood in *Metamorphoses*, Book I, Milton describes the ending of a world for all but a select group who maintained their faithfulness despite opposition and ridicule. Adam's reaction, again wrong, is abject despair, for it seems to him that peace corrupts people, through self-indulgence, as much as war wastes them (XI. 784). The future for everyone, he feels, seems to be unavoidably bad, so we are helplessly locked in misery and may as well forget the future. Michael's corrective to this determinist way of thinking is to give an account that reads as if it is Milton's disillusionment with English political leaders in the 1650s being redeemed by the 'one just man' of integrity:

Those whom last thou saw'st
In triumph and luxurious wealth, are they
First seen in acts of prowess eminent
And great exploits, but of true virtue void;

Who having spilt much blood, and done much waste
Subduing nations, and achieved thereby
Fame in the world, high titles, and rich prey,
Shall change their course to pleasure, ease, and sloth,
Surfeit, and lust, till wantonness and pride
Raise out of friendship hostile deeds in peace.
The conquered also, and enslaved by war
Shall with their freedom lost all virtue lose
And fear of God . . .
So all shall turn degenerate, all depraved,
Justice and temperance, truth and faith forgot;
One man except, the only son of light
In a dark age, against example good,
Against allurement, custom, and a world
Offended; fearless of reproach and scorn,
Or violence, he of their wicked ways
Shall them admonish, and before them set
The paths of righteousness.

(XI. 787–99, 806–14)

Enoch, Noah, Milton: all demonstrated the 'better fortitude/Of patience and heroic martyrdom' (IX. 31–2). Michael describes how the Flood destroys the literal Paradise in Eden, which becomes a barren island in the Persian Gulf.

The sixth and last episode in Michael's scenario shows the Flood receding and Noah and his family stepping out of the ark on to dry land, with the rainbow above them as token of God's promise that he would never again destroy mankind. Adam is revived by the sight, and rejoices for 'one man found so perfect and so just' as Noah (XI. 876). Adam needed to learn the lesson of repentance in Book X. Now in Book XI he has learned the lessons of patience, moderation, and endurance, as the first two thousand years or so of human history conclude, on a positive note, with mankind entering a new era.

3 Michael's Account of History, from Nimrod to the Second Coming: XII. 1–551

Just as we, the readers of *Paradise Lost*, have followed a narrative of events designed to justify to us God's ways to men, so Adam now hears Michael's account of the pattern of history and learns the lesson explicitly acknowledged at the end. Augustine's massive work, *City of God*, had also attempted to show a divine pattern in human history, and it concluded with a condensation of that history into six epochs:

1. from Adam to the Flood;
2. from the Flood to Abraham;
3. from Abraham to David;
4. from David to the Exile in Babylon;
5. from the Exile to the Coming of Christ in the flesh;
6. the Present Age (to the Second Coming of Christ).[5]

This is the pattern adopted, more or less, by Milton. The story of the first epoch was presented to Adam in a series of scenes in Book XI: the next five epochs are now episodically described by Michael, since Adam's 'mortal sight' begins to fail because of the strain on him (XII. 9). The major objective of the narrative is to drive home the lesson of how to behave in a fallen world, the lesson that Milton himself had derived from a consideration of the failures of God's chosen nation, the English, in recent years. The narrative also, however, introduces a number of kings and leaders who can be understood to be 'shadows', or 'types', of Christ, the heavenly king, as well as two tyrants, who earn God's disapproval.

The first part of Michael's narrative concerns the second epoch, from the Flood to Abraham. Mankind is at first righteous and prosperous, under a benevolent, paternal governorship, but this state does not last long:

> *One shall rise*
> *Of proud ambitious heart, who not content*
> *With fair equality, fraternal state,*
> *Will arrogate dominion undeserved*
> *Over his brethren, and quite dispossess*
> *Concord and law of nature from the earth,*
> *Hunting (and men not beasts shall be his game)*
> *With war and hostile snare such as refuse*
> *Subjection to his empire tyrannous.*
>
> (XII. 24–32)

This is Nimrod, the first king. In the description here of a movement from 'fraternal state' to 'dominion' and 'empire tyrannous', motivated by pride and ambition, we can see Milton's own strong republican sentiments being justified. In his pamphlet, *The Tenure of Kings and Magistrates*, published a fortnight after the execution of Charles I in 1649, Milton had forcibly argued that kings have no divine right, but that their power is 'only derivative, transferr'd and committed to them in trust from the People, to the common good of them all, in whom the power yet remaines fundamentally'.[6] Nimrod, however, with a 'proud ambitious heart' like Satan, is a mighty hunter 'before the Lord', which could either mean 'in defiance of the Lord', or, alternatively, 'claiming sovereignty from the Lord'. Even the latter for Milton is unacceptable: in the same pamphlet he had written that 'to say Kings are accountable to none but God, is the overturning of all law and government'.[7] Nimrod builds the Tower of Babel in order to ensure the lasting fame of himself and his people, but God, seeing the Tower as a potential challenge and obstruction of the towers of heaven, confuses their language, so that, unable to understand each other, their ambitions are frustrated. Adam's observation that Nimrod's authority was not God-given – 'man over men/He made not lord' – prompts from Michael the argument that the psychological tyranny of passion in the individual leads to political tyranny in society at large (XII. 69–70). The basis for the argument is Milton's long-held view that 'none can love freedom heartilie but good men; the rest love not freedom but licence; which never hath more scope or more indulgence then under Tyrants'.[8] Here Michael tells Adam that 'since thy original lapse, true liberty/Is lost, which always with right reason [i.e. 'conscience'] dwells/Twinned' (XII. 83–5). This is Milton's faith, that liberty, or free will, together with 'right reason', produce virtue, when not subverted by 'upstart passions'. When such subversion takes place it has political consequences, as Milton explains in what is one of the key passages for understanding the whole poem:

> *Reason in man obscured, or not obeyed,*
> *Immediately inordinate desires*
> *And upstart passions catch the government*
> *From reason, and to servitude reduce*
> *Man till then free. Therefore since he permits*
> *Within himself unworthy powers to reign*
> *Over free reason, God in judgment just*
> *Subjects him from without to violent lords;*
> *Who oft as undeservedly enthral*
> *His outward freedom: tyranny must be,*
> *Though to the tyrant thereby no excuse.*
> *Yet sometimes nations will decline so low*
> *From virtue, which is reason, that no wrong,*
> *But justice, and some fatal curse annexed*

Deprives them of their outward liberty,
Their inward lost.

(XII. 86–101)

This begins to account for the failure of the English Revolution in the 1650s: it was the loss of individual 'inward' liberty, through departure from reason, or virtue, which led to the social and political failure. The solution is the hard road of individual struggle, for which Adam is now being trained.

We have seen one new 'beginning' for mankind so far, after the Flood. In the third epoch of human history we see another sort of new beginning in God's selection of a 'chosen nation' to derive from 'one faithful man', Abraham (XII. 113). He is obedient to God's command to go to a new land, as Adam will shortly have to, and the point is emphasized, in explanation of the curse on the serpent, that it is by Abraham's 'seed' that all nations of the earth will be blessed (X. 181; XII. 147–8). His descendants grow to be a nation within Egypt, and are eventually enslaved by a vengeful Pharaoh who also kills their male children. (This Pharaoh was named Busiris in a simile in I. 307.) The plagues sent by God upon Egypt cause him to release the Israelites, but his heart is 'stubborn', and he is eventually destroyed in the Red Sea, after the Israelites are led through by Moses, who miraculously parts and closes the sea (XII. 193). Moses becomes the 'mediator' between God and the nation of Israel during their wanderings in the wilderness, and himself comes to foreshadow Christ, the 'greater man' referred to at the opening of the poem (I. 4; XII. 240, 242). Eventually, after many years, they settle in the promised land of Canaan. Adam, ironically, at this point claims to find his 'eyes true opening' (which was the unfulfilled promise of the serpent in IX. 705–9) and jumps to the wrong conclusion that it is in the Israelite nation, as the 'seed' of Abraham, that 'all nations shall be blest' (XII. 274, 277). Michael then explains that God's laws given to the Israelites through Moses, and his 'covenant' or agreement with them, merely foreshadow a greater covenant with mankind based not on 'law', which can 'discover sin, but not remove', but on faith (XII. 290, 306). Moses, therefore, 'the minister/Of law', did not lead his people into the promised land: that task was given to Joshua, 'whom the gentiles Jesus call', and who is a type of Christ, who will 'bring back/Through the world's wilderness long wandered man/Safe to eternal paradise of rest' (XII. 308–14). Everything now looks forward to Christ.

The fourth epoch of history introduces King David, yet another ancestor and type of the 'seed' of the prophecy. His rule is followed by a degeneration, which results in captivity for the Israelites in Babylon, and, eventually, after religious dissension, in the loss of the throne 'to a stranger, that the true/Anointed king Messiah might be born/Barred of his right' (XII. 358–60). Michael continues:

> *A virgin is his mother, but his sire*
> *The power of the most high; he shall ascend*
> *The throne hereditary, and bound his reign*
> *With earth's wide bounds, his glory with the heavens.*
>
> (XII. 368–71)

On hearing this, Adam cries with 'joy/Surcharged', since he now understands how 'God with man unites' (XII. 372–3, 382). This is the high point of Augustine's fifth epoch, which Milton has joined to the fourth, in order to leave the fifth concerned entirely with the death and resurrection of Christ.

The bruising of Satan's head, Michael explains, is not a matter of Christ destroying Satan, but of destroying 'his works/In thee and in thy seed' (X. 181; XII. 394–5). This is accomplished by Christ's obedience to God, which compensates for Adam's disobedience (XII. 397). Christ's obedience, to the extent of suffering death, the penalty incurred by Adam, satisfies 'high justice', and 'proclaims life' to all believers, imputed to them through their faith, rather than through their own works (XII. 401, 407, 410). With him dies the law of Moses, and the sins of all mankind, but he is then brought back to life, having thus redeemed man:

> *... this Godlike act*
> *Annuls thy doom, the death thou shouldst have died,*
> *In sin for ever lost from life; this act*
> *Shall bruise the head of Satan, crush his strength*
> *Defeating Sin and Death, his two main arms,*
> *And fix far deeper in his head their stings*
> *Than temporal death shall bruise the victor's heel,*
> *Or theirs whom he redeems, a death like sleep,*
> *A gentle wafting to immortal life.*
>
> (XII. 427–35)

Thus, finally, is the full meaning of the mysterious prophecy revealed to Adam. This redemption will apply to all those 'of Abraham's faith wherever through the world;/So in his seed all nations shall be blest' (XII. 449–50). Eventually, at his second coming on judgment day, the Messiah will reward the faithful and

. . . receive them into bliss,
Whether in heaven or earth, for then the earth
Shall all be paradise, far happier place
Than this of Eden, and far happier days.

(XII. 462–5)

Near the start of the poem, Satan's second speech on the burning lake had included this undertaking:

If then his providence
Out of our evil seek to bring forth good,
Our labour must be to pervert that end,
And out of good still to find means of evil.

(I. 162–5)

Satan will clearly have failed: and now Adam succinctly articulates the paradox of the Fortunate Fall, which is the positive inspiration for the whole poem:

O goodness infinite, goodness immense!
That all this good of evil shall produce,
And evil turn to good; more wonderful
Than that which by creation first brought forth
Light out of darkness! Full of doubt I stand,
Whether I should repent me now of sin
By me done and occasioned, or rejoice
Much more, that much more good thereof shall spring,
To God more glory, more good will to men
From God, and over wrath grace shall abound.

(XII. 469–78)

The paradox is in Adam's question, as to whether he should repent or rejoice, since as a result of his disobedience so much good is to come about that would not otherwise have done. There is still suffering to come for the faithful, however, though this will be recompensed with 'inward consolations' as a result of the sending of the 'Comforter', or Holy Spirit (XII. 486, 495). The forecast of the future corruption of the Church allows Milton to revive the message of his pamphlet attacks on the prelatical Church of England and on the Church of Rome.[9] Here Michael forecasts the entry of 'wolves', into the flock, who will turn religion to their own advantage, and not only take secular power, but also appropriate to themselves religious prerogatives which are 'promised alike and given/To all believers' (XII. 508, 519–20). In true radical Protestant style, Michael argues for the supreme arbitration of individual conscience, unmediated by an elite group of 'bishops': 'Who against faith and conscience can be heard/Infallible?' (XII. 529–30). The answer is that many will try. As a result:

> *... heavy persecution shall arise*
> *On all who in the worship persevere*
> *Of spirit and truth; the rest, far greater part,*
> *Will deem in outward rites and specious forms*
> *Religion satisfied; truth shall retire*
> *Bestuck with slanderous darts, and works of faith*
> *Rarely be found: so shall the world go on,*
> *To good malignant, to bad men benign,*
> *Under her own weight groaning till the day*
> *Appear of respiration* [i.e. 'rest'] *to the just.*
>
> (XII. 531–40)

This is the world of failure which Milton knew, and which began with the 'groans' of nature at the Fall – the world in which a 'fit audience' for these unpalatable truths is 'few' (IX. 783, 1001; VII. 31). The final resolution of human history entails the dissolution of Satan, and the emergence of 'new heavens, new earth' at the Second Coming, which will be 'Founded in righteousness and peace and love/To bring forth fruits joy and eternal bliss' (XII. 549–51). So the bitter fruit of the first line of the poem is here changed to the sweet fruits of joy and bliss eternally.

4 The Eviction of Adam and Eve from Paradise: XII. 552–649

What has Adam learned from his visions and from Michael's narrative? In two words, the importance of obedience and 'fortitude' (XII. 570). Obedience, in Milton's definition, is far from passive acquiescence to power. The conscience is the location of 'right reason', and willingly obeying 'right reason' is what makes a person virtuous and therefore truly free (VI. 42; XII. 84, 98). Obedience to the dictates of right reason therefore is a radical force in the world – 'by things deemed weak/Subverting worldly strong, and worldly wise/By simply meek' (XII. 567–9). Adam now has peace of mind, knowing his place in the scheme of things, and understanding the need for strenuous struggle. This is the 'sum/Of wisdom', and exceeds in value all scientific knowledge of the secrets of nature, all wealth and all worldly power (XII. 575–6). With faith, virtue, patience, temperance, and love, Michael tells Adam,

> *... then wilt thou not be loath*
> *To leave this Paradise, but shalt possess*
> *A paradise within thee, happier far.*
>
> (XII. 585–7)

The 'hell within' of Satan is the alternative to the love, joy, and peace, the 'paradise within', of which fallen mankind is still capable (IV. 20, 75).

It is now noon, 'the hour precise', for the expulsion from Paradise. Noon was the time of the Fall, but also of the crucifixion, so this moment of losing Paradise not only fulfils the literal terms of the prohibition – 'the day thou eat'st thereof ... from that day mortal' (VIII. 329–31) – but also looks forward to the redemption of mankind symbolized by the crucifixion. Michael had put Eve to sleep 'with gentle dreams' before the visions in Book XI, and now he sends Adam to wake her (XI. 367; XII. 594). Thus a positive though sad mood emerges at the climax of the poem. Adam and Eve together are at peace for the first time since the Fall, and are comforted by the promise of the 'seed', the full understanding of which it is Adam's commission to explain to Eve (XII. 600). She now says to Adam:

> *... thou to me*
> *Art all things under heaven, all places thou,*
> *Who for my wilful crime art banished hence.*
> *This further consolation yet secure*
> *I carry hence; though all by me is lost,*
> *Such favour I unworthy am vouchsafed,*
> *By me the promised seed shall all restore.*
>
> (XII. 617–23)

These, the last words spoken by Adam or Eve, are fittingly positive. They have come a long way since their creation a fortnight or so earlier, but they have the major journey of their life yet to make. As they are led down from Paradise to the plain below, with the flaming sword behind them beginning to 'parch that temperate clime', they look back momentarily (XII. 636). Their tears are brief, as their great task awaits them:

> *The world was all before them, where to choose*
> *Their place of rest, and providence their guide:*
> *They hand in hand with wandering steps and slow,*
> *Through Eden took their solitary way.*
>
> (XII. 646–9)

Their way is 'solitary', even though they go 'hand in hand', and they have 'providence' as their guide, though the ambiguous syntax implies that this is only if they so choose. The future is now a matter of struggle, and of real choices, with a 'paradise within' to sustain them if they make the right ones.

'The problem most in need of solution in the sixties was how good men fail, how people with the right ideas come to make the wrong choices', writes Christopher Hill.[10] Milton accepted that the English had been the people chosen by God to lead the Reformation, through the agency of Wycliffe: 'England', he wrote, 'had this grace and honour from God to bee the first that should set up a standard for the recovery of lost truth.'[11] The failure of the English Revolution, which he had once seen as a continuation of God's favour on the English, had caused him to question 'divine providence' in a fundamental way. *Paradise Lost* is the result, and the poem suggests that the problem and its solution lie with the individual, in individual struggle and choice. Milton says, with God, that 'they themselves ordained their fall' (III. 128). There were not enough good individuals in the 1650s worthy of freedom, since, we remember, only 'good men' can 'love freedom heartilie'.[12] So the reconstruction of individuals in accordance with the dictates of 'right reason' has become the programme which Milton proposes, in which 'inner', or psychological change is a precondition for 'outer', or social and political change. This involves a big readjustment in the time-scale for God's purposes to be fulfilled, but in the end Milton has confirmed confidence in eternal providence, and believes that, given individual reformation, the pattern of history will be justified.

References

I Preliminaries

1. See A. O. Lovejoy, 'Milton and the Paradox of the Fortunate Fall', *ELH*, 4 (1937), 161–79.
2. John Dryden, 'Dedication of the Aeneis' (1697); William Blake, *The Marriage of Heaven and Hell* (1790); Percy Bysshe Shelley, *A Defence of Poetry* (1821).
3. Blake, *The Marriage of Heaven and Hell*.
4. William Empson, *Milton's God* (Cambridge, 1965), p. 83.
5. *The Life Records of John Milton*, ed. J. M. French (N.J., 1949–58), II, 413.
6. *John Milton: Selected Prose*, ed. C. A. Patrides (Penguin, 1974), p. 82.
7. ibid., p. 71.
8. ibid., p. 230.
9. ibid., p. 72.
10. 'On the New Forcers of Conscience under the Long Parliament'.
11. *John Milton: Selected Prose*, pp. 236–7.
12. Christopher Hill, *Milton and the English Revolution* (Faber, 1977), p. 347.
13. *John Milton: Selected Prose*, p. 349.
14. Keith Thomas, *Religion and the Decline of Magic* (Penguin, 1973), p. 105.
15. ibid., p. 510.

II The First Day: Hell, and Satan's Journey

1. John Milton, *De Doctrina Christiana*, I.6.
2. *Seventeenth-century England: A Changing Culture*, ed. Ann Hughes, Vol. I (Ward Lock/OUP, 1980), pp. 330, 335.
3. Milton's note on 'The Verse', added in the second edition.
4. *John Milton: Selected Prose*, pp. 212–13.
5. ibid., p. 263.
6. Christopher Ricks, *Milton's Grand Style* (Oxford, 1963), pp. 159–60.
7. Empson, *Milton's God*, p. 124.
8. John Locke, *Two Treatises of Government*, II.9.
9. Homer, *Iliad*, trans. E. V. Rieu (Penguin, 1950), p. 38.
10. *The 'Metamorphoses' of Ovid*, trans. M. M. Innes (Penguin, 1955), pp. 32–3.
11. Homer, *Iliad*, p. 38.
12. Ricks, *Milton's Grand Style*, p. 15.
13. *Puritanism and Liberty: Being the Army Debates (1647–9) from the Clarke Manuscripts*, ed. A. S. P. Woodhouse (London, 1965).
14. *John Milton: Selected Prose*, p. 336.
15. Empson, *Milton's God*, pp. 48–53.
16. ibid., p. 118.
17. Dennis Danielson, *Milton's Good God* (Cambridge, 1982), pp. 50, 51, 57.

III The Second Day: Heaven, Satan's Journey, and Paradise

1. Anne Ferry, *Milton's Epic Voice: the Narrator in 'Paradise Lost'*, 2nd edn. (Chicago, 1983), p. 47.
2. Empson, *Milton's God*, p. 146.
3. See, e.g., Pope, 'Epistle to Burlington' (1731).
4. See C. B. Macpherson, *The Political Theory of Possessive Individualism: Hobbes to Locke* (Oxford, 1962), p. 282; also his defence of the same argument in *Democratic Theory* (Oxford, 1973), pp. 207–24.
5. Macpherson, *The Political Theory of Possessive Individualism*, p. 123.
6. ibid., p. 296.
7. Lawrence Stone, *The Family, Sex and Marriage in England 1500–1800*, abridged edn. (Penguin, 1979), p. 217.
8. Keith Wrightson, *English Society 1580–1680* (Hutchinson, 1982), p. 104; see also Ralph Houlbrooke, *The English Family 1450–1700* (Longman, 1984), p. 98.
9. *John Milton: Selected Prose*, p. 124.
10. ibid., p. 136.
11. See R. H. Tawney, *Religion and the Rise of Capitalism* (Penguin, 1938), pp. 240ff.
12. Houlbrooke, *The English Family 1450–1700*, p. 107.
13. See *The 'Metamorphoses' of Ovid*, III, 402ff.
14. Houlbrooke, *The English Family 1450–1700*, p. 98.
15. Stone, *The Family, Sex and Marriage in England 1500–1800*, pp. 313ff.
16. See Empson, *Milton's God*, pp. 112–14.

IV The Third Day: Paradise – the Lunch-Party Conversation

1. Stone, *The Family, Sex and Marriage in England 1500–1800*, p. 220.
2. *John Milton: Selected Prose*, p. 249.
3. Augustine, *City of God*, trans. Henry Bettenson (Penguin, 1972), p. 571.
4. Empson, *Milton's God*, p. 97.
5. *John Milton: Selected Prose*, pp. 255, 259.
6. Augustine, *City of God*, pp. 572–3.
7. C. S. Lewis, *A Preface to 'Paradise Lost'* (Oxford, 1960), p. 112.
8. Sergei Eisenstein, *The Film Sense*, trans. Jay Leyda (Faber, 1968), pp. 54ff. The passages he quotes and analyses are VI. 78–86, 231–46, 853–71.
9. *John Milton: Selected Prose*, p. 373.
10. Ricks, *Milton's Grand Style*, pp. 98–9.
11. William Wordsworth, *The Prelude* (1805 edn.), X. 892–900.
12. *John Milton: Selected Prose*, pp. 135–6.

V The Fourth Day: Paradise – One Week Later

1. See Ricks, *Milton's Grand Style*, pp. 144–7.

2. *John Milton: Selected Prose*, pp. 213, 220.
3. ibid., p. 211.
4. Stone, *The Family, Sex and Marriage in England 1500–1800*, p. 153.
5. Empson, *Milton's God*, p. 117.
6. Homer, *Odyssey*, XIII.
7. Milton, *De Doctrina Christiana*, I.19.
8. *John Milton: Selected Prose*, pp. 387–9.

VI The Fifth Day: Paradise Lost and the Consequences

1. See Thomas, *Religion and the Decline of Magic*, pp. 103–6.
2. See Raymond Williams, *The Country and the City* (Paladin, 1975).
3. Thomas, *Religion and the Decline of Magic*, pp. 54, 87, 88.
4. Genesis 5:21–4; Hebrews 11:5.
5. Augustine, *City of God*, p. 1091.
6. *John Milton: Selected Prose*, p. 257.
7. ibid., p. 258.
8. ibid., p. 249.
9. e.g. *Of Reformation touching Church-Discipline*, in *John Milton: Selected Prose*, pp. 77–111.
10. Hill, *Milton and the English Revolution*, p. 349.
11. *John Milton: Selected Prose*, p. 81.
12. ibid., p. 249.

Further Reading

The best available edition of *Paradise Lost*, which has been used in this study, is *Paradise Lost*, ed. Alastair Fowler (Longman, 1971). It is a fully annotated paperback, with an informative introduction. Its companion volume, *John Milton: Complete Shorter Poems*, ed. John Carey (Longman, 1971), is equally scholarly and useful.

An excellent way to start a study of Milton is to get *John Milton: Selected Prose*, ed. C. A. Patrides (Penguin, 1974). This contains the best of Milton's English prose, together with a useful introduction, biographical outline, Milton's autobiographical pieces, and two early biographies, by John Aubrey and Edward Phillips, Milton's nephew. A popular modern biography is A. N. Wilson, *The Life of John Milton* (Oxford, 1984).

For a picture of Milton and a reading of his works in a historical context, the best book by far is Christopher Hill, *Milton and the English Revolution* (Faber, 1977); though, if you can find it, it is also useful to read the critique of Hill's book contained in Andrew Milner, *John Milton and the English Revolution* (Macmillan, 1981), which is by a sociologist rather than a historian.

For a Christian approach to the poem which places it in its literary context, C. S. Lewis, *A Preface to 'Paradise Lost'* (Oxford paperback, 1960), is still useful. William Empson's controversial but brilliant *Milton's God* (Cambridge, 1981) is a sympathetic atheist's view of the poem, and highly recommended. Alastair Fowler's edition, mentioned above, spends some time in footnotes attempting to refute Empson.

The best appreciation of Milton's poetic style is Christopher Ricks, *Milton's Grand Style* (Oxford, 1963), and a good general introduction to epic is C. M. Bowra, *From Virgil to Milton* (Macmillan, 1948).

The first three editions mentioned above all have excellent bibliographies for yet further reading, and a visit to any good library will reveal a selection of the numerous books on Milton and on *Paradise Lost*, and editions of the poem or parts of the poem. In particular, Dennis Burden, *The Logical Epic* (RKP, 1967), and B. Rajan, *'Paradise Lost' and the Seventeenth Century Reader* (Chatto & Windus, 1947), are clear and informative.

PENGUIN CLASSICS

ANTHOLOGIES AND ANONYMOUS WORKS

The Age of Bede
Alfred the Great
Beowulf
A Celtic Miscellany
The Cloud of Unknowing and Other Works
The Death of King Arthur
The Earliest English Poems
Early Christian Writings
Early Irish Myths and Sagas
Egil's Saga
King Arthur's Death
The Letters of Abelard and Heloise
Medieval English Verse
Njal's Saga
Seven Viking Romances
Sir Gawain and the Green Knight
The Song of Roland